JAGUAR
XK8

THE AUTHORISED BIOGRAPHY
BY PHILIP PORTER

EDITED BY MARK HUGHES

IN ASSOCIATION WITH PORTER & PORTER LTD

Published 1996 by
Bay View Books Ltd
The Red House
25-26 Bridgeland Street
Bideford
Devon EX39 2PZ

© Copyright 1996 by
Philip Porter
Designed by Bruce Aiken
Special photography by
Peter Burn, Mike Cann,
Roger Clinkscales and
Paul Debois.

ISBN 1 870979 75 3

Printed in Hong Kong
by Paramount Printing Co.

CONTENTS

INTRODUCTION

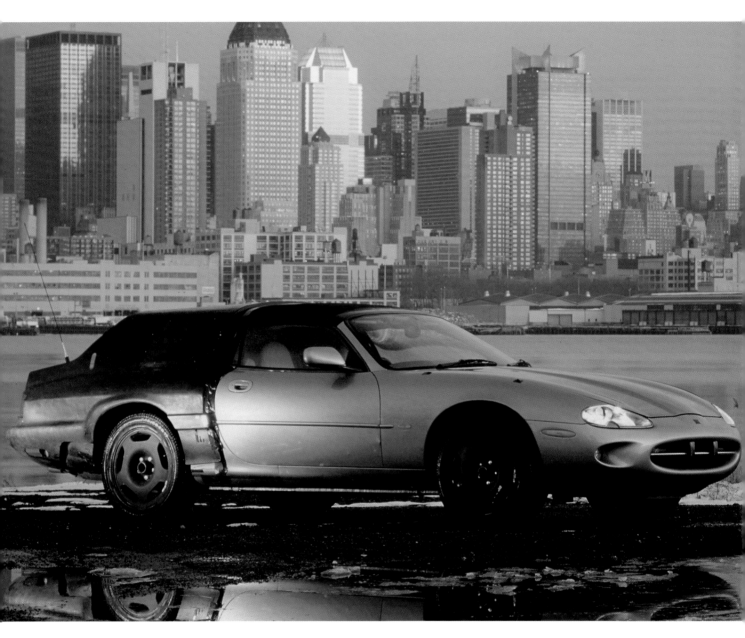

Between these covers you will find a full and frank account of the Jaguar XK8 story. As well as looking at the background, design, development, production, launch and marketing of an exciting new sports car, the book concurrently charts the rebirth of Jaguar as a vibrant and successful force in the automotive world.

For five months I lived and breathed virtually nothing but XK8. The idea for this book, which has been timed to coincide with the XK8's launch, came from David Boole, Jaguar's Director of Public Relations. I had known of his excitement about the XK8 for some time, and he gave me the go-ahead to get under the skin of the pro-

ject in late 1995. But I turned up for my first meeting with David and Chief Programme Engineer Bob Dover to learn that David had tragically died during the night. In many of my subsequent interviews with senior personnel, they often made the same point. David had always been forthright in his views that Jaguar had to preserve and maintain its wonderful heritage and unique niche. Like so many, he gave body and soul to the company.

This dedication to the spirit of Jaguar is something that was prevalent in the fifties and sixties and beyond, but it is most encouraging to know that the same level of loyal commitment runs deeper than ever through this

account is a distillation of over 150 hours of interviews and discussion.

To write this book, I have had to learn a new language! It might be termed Jaguar Speak. Like many languages, it is living, ever-changing, full of jargon and liberally spiced with acronyms. The specialised vocabulary seems endless, but I have attempted to avoid the unintelligible wherever possible, and to assist the reader I have compiled a glossary that appears on page 128.

As for the illustration, I am particularly delighted to have worked with Peter Burn, Mike Cann, Roger Clinkscales and Paul Debois – four of Britain's top car photographers. The excellence of their work adds immeasurably to this book. There are also archive shots of models never before published, and Jaguar has kindly released the very first official shots ever to be seen of the XJ41, or F-type as it is often called.

That the XK120 and E-type were sensational success stories is fact. To have been involved so closely with the team that created Jaguar's third great sports car has been an enormous privilege. Neither the team, nor their senior colleagues who have guided the company back to success, have held anything back. I have been party to everything, however sensitive, in order to produce the most candid, behind-the-scenes account. It has been a complex exercise involving many people who have taken enormous time and trouble.

These two scenes were only a couple of months apart. A Verification Prototype (VP) pauses in New York while, on the other side of the Atlantic, the author tests a Functional Build (FB) car.

emotive company. The latest XJ saloons (X300) have turned the company round, the XK8 (X100) will rekindle the passions, and the forthcoming high-volume small saloon (X200) should capitalise upon this solid progress. So Jaguar has a future once more and everyone, from shop floor to board room, is buzzing with genuine excitement.

As is usual with my books, I have chosen to tell much of this fascinating story in the words of the people involved. Paradoxically this approach does not make the task any easier, but I believe it makes for a much more readable, pithy and, at times, humorous book. This

The emotion within Jaguar has rubbed off on me. I felt highly honoured to be the first 'outsider' to drive the XK8, and my enthusiasm gradually transformed into passion. I am fortunate to own several older Jaguar sports cars, and one day I hope to be able to park an XK8 alongside them. Like the XKs and E-types, the XK8 is surely destined to go down as another great Jaguar sports car.

Philip Porter
Knighton-on-Teme, Worcestershire, June 1996

ACKNOWLEDGEMENTS

I should like both to acknowledge my very grateful thanks to the following and to give an indication of their role in the creation of the XK8.

Nick Scheele	Chairman

Maurice Arnett	Principal Engineer, Electrical Engineering
Mike Beasley	Director, Manufacturing Operations
Liam Brown	Principal Engineer, Electrical Engineering
Tony Cartwright	Manager, Ride, Handling & Refinement
Trevor Crisp	Group Chief Engineer, Power Unit & Transmissions
Mike Cross	Principal Engineer, Ride & Handling
Mike Dale	President, Jaguar Cars Inc (US)
Bob Dover	Chief Programme Engineer, Sports Cars
Clive Ennos	Director, Production Engineering Operations
Nick Gilkes	Senior Engineer, Vehicle Refinement & Testing
Joe Greenwell	Director, Communications & Public Affairs
Ken Heap	Manager, Suspension & Braking Systems
Paul Heynes	Principal Engineer, Trim Engineering
David Hudson	Director, Production Operations
Richard Ingram	Business Director
Jeffrey Key	Manager, Vehicle Launch
Manfred Lampe	Director, Design Process & Development
Geoff Lawson	Styling Director
Jim Padilla	Executive Director, Engineering & Manufacturing (later Performance Luxury Vehicle Line Director, Ford Motor Company)
Roger Putnam	Director, Sales & Marketing
Paul Stokes	Supply Director (later Director, Rear Wheel Drive Vehicle Centre Purchasing, Ford Motor Company)
David Szczupak	Chief Engineer, Power Unit
Colin Tivey	Chief Engineer, Launch Team
Keith Turfrey	Manager, Transmission & Axle Development
Paul Walker	Chief Engineer, Vehicle & Chassis Engineering

X100 PROJECT TEAM MEMBERS

Keith Adams	Timing
Richard Ansell	Sales, Marketing & Service
Chris Bevan	Manufacturing Engineering
Tim Brear	Manufacturing
Martin Broomer	Sports Car Programme Office Manager & Concept Project Manager (later Manager, Product Affairs, PR Office)
Tony Duckhouse	Finance Manager, X100
Pete French	Powertrain Engineering
Phil Hodgkinson	Sports Car Programme Office Manager (later Launch Team Manager)
Julian Jenkins	Sports Car Programme Office – Body, Trim & Electrical
Mandy John	Timing, X100
Paul Johnson	BIW Prototype Manufacture (later Launch Manager)
Umit Koymen	Body Construction Manager
Chris Leadbeater	X100 Convertible Programme Manager (later Sports Car Vehicle Office Manager)
Ian Minards	Prototype Build (later member of Launch Team)
Andy Murphy	Chassis Design Co-ordinator, X100
Ian Parker	Engineering Quality, X100
Fergus Pollock	Styling Manager, X100
Mark Poole	Electrical Engineering, X100
Kevin Riches	BIW and Trim Engineering (assisted by Helen Atkins)
Nigel Sims	BIW Tooling, X100
Russ Varney	Vehicle Office (later Sports Car Programme Manager)
Jonathan Wankling	Programme Office – Chassis & Powertrain
Mark White	BIW, X100
David Williams	Purchasing Manager, X100

The following have also very kindly given assistance: Ayub Bhayat, Amanda Broadhurst, John Burinshaw, Dave Crisp, Jennie David, Alan Hodge, Tim Nelmes, Sharon Park, Bill Prickett, Linda Ralph, Chris Scott, Hilary Seedhouse, Cecile Simon and Stuart Spencer.

Allison Simpkins, assistant to Bob Dover and David Scholes, helped me enormously by arranging interviews, planning my diary and cheerfully putting up with my many tedious requests. Ian Minards assisted greatly in arranging photography of prototypes and cars to borrow when they were very scarce. Russ Varney was especially helpful with photographs, particularly in organising work at MIRA. Nick Gilkes could not have done more to assist at MIRA. Jonathan Wankling kindly arranged various photographs and generally assisted. Fergus Pollock guided me, more than once, through the styling story and organised the styling illustrations.

In the PR office Bridget Tedds, as ever, was a tower of strength. Martin Broomer, in spite of many calls on his time during a very hectic period, played a major role. Joe Greenwell, who took over from David Boole in sad circumstances, lent his enthusiastic support and gave much good advice. Ann Harris of the Jaguar Daimler Heritage Trust was most helpful.

I would like to express my gratitude to Jaguar for providing so many of the illustrations. Additional thanks must also go to John Lowe of Warwicks UK Ltd, J. Walter Thompson, John Colley Photographic and Stan Papior of *Autocar* magazine.

I should also like to thank Mark Hughes, who has edited this book and helped in a million different ways. During an enormously pressured spell when I had to work very long hours, Mark gave his usual tremendous support and the book benefits from his great professionalism. Charles Herridge, my co-publisher, was closely involved at all stages, giving wise counsel and kind support. Writing a book on a subject of this complexity in five months was not easy and I most certainly could not have done it without my wife Julie's total – and incredibly unselfish – support.

Finally, I should like to thank the man whose baby the whole XK8 project has been. Bob Dover has given me copious information from many sources including his own diaries, lent his photographs, encouraged people to help and given wonderful support. Bob has dedicated the past few years to driving the XK8 project, but he would be the first to say that it has been a team effort with other senior colleagues and his Project Team. He particularly wished to add this personal tribute to his colleagues.

'Developing a car from concept to production is a team effort, and I am proud to have led the XK8 Project Team. In a book of this kind, it is impossible to mention everyone who has played a part, but, from a personal perspective, the commitment of all the people involved in meeting tough objectives has been outstanding. Whether as representatives of each of the company functions, as members of the Project Team, the Launch Team, or as one of our supplier partners, the credit for the success of the programme is theirs.

The story of the XK8 is also the latest chapter in the story of the renaissance of Jaguar. The lessons learned in delivering the XJ range of saloons were all applied to the XK8 development planning. As a result, the XK8 has been delivered ahead of time and in line with all the objectives set for the team when formal approval was given in December 1993.

The XK8 story has been a triumph for team and process management. To put the achievement in context, the XK8 is the most complex as well as the fastest major programme achieved by Jaguar – with new bodyshells, new powertrains and electronics.

Jaguar's heritage is important to all of us who work in the company. It sets us apart from our competitors. It is a touchstone when we make decisions that affect styling, performance and refinement.

We need, however, to build on our heritage. You will remember some of the great Jaguar products of the past, but our goal is to be known for the outstanding products we are making now. The XK8 is the latest in a line of cars in which we take real pride.'

Bob Dover

DRIVING THE JAGUAR XK8

S tunning. Sensational. Awesome. These are a few of the words that come to mind when you drive the new Jaguar XK8.

It is a breathtakingly superb motor car. Behind the wheel you immediately sense that the car has been brilliantly engineered in every facet, from the minor details to the total execution. It is impossible to avoid a cliché – the car undoubtedly sets new standards.

I find the XK8 utterly intoxicating. More than that, it is addictive, whether you are gazing at its feline grace or experiencing the excitement of driving it. This is a true Jaguar, of that there is no question. I own an XK120 Roadster and an early E-type, and I use them both. The XK was brilliant in the fifties, the E-type stunning in the sixties. The XK8 is true to the tradition. Once again it rocks the competition, once again it will be the yardstick.

But the XK8 is more than a great successor in the same mould. In truth, the E-type could be criticised for its brakes, which is ironic considering that Jaguar pioneered the use of disc brakes in motor racing. It could be criticised for its poor seats and slow gearbox, but in those days the press and enthusiastic owners were more tolerant, and furthermore the E-type was such a startling revelation in almost every other way. That the E-type overheated dreadfully and was embarrassingly unreliable in hotter climates cannot be denied, even if most of these matters were gradually addressed.

Today such tolerance is not remotely on the agenda. The XK8 makes few compromises. There is no area where the engineers have accepted second best. A word

that appears often throughout this story, and is much used by Jaguar engineers, is benchmark: something which serves as a standard from which others may be measured. Thus if you benchmark the best car in its class for power, you would find it to be the BMW 8-series – until now. If you benchmark the best in class for refinement, you would discover it to be the Lexus – until now.

The Jaguar engineers have benchmarked the competition in every component and sphere imaginable. Sometimes the best was the car the XK8 was replacing, the XJS. Often it was the Lexus Coupé, the SL Mercedes, the larger BMWs, the Porsches. Naturally, some are stronger in one area and weaker in another. All are very fine cars in many ways. But Jaguar set out to equal, and as often as possible, exceed the best aspects of each of the competition. Thus by definition the sum of the parts of the XK8 must considerably exceed the sum of the parts of its counterparts. And this is largely based on measurable criteria.

That is the theory. In the early part of 1996, I drove all the competitors to establish my own set of benchmarks. A little later I also tried several of the XK8 prototypes that will be described in later chapters, to understand how Jaguar had approached the challenge and then honed the concept. And then one May afternoon, some five months before the car was due to be launched, I glided out of the Jaguar factory gates in a still secret XK8 Coupé.

The first thing I always notice about a Jaguar is its quietness. Refinement has traditionally been a great

The Jaguar XK8 overtakes the competition on performance, refinement and style. It is destined to power Jaguar through to the next millennium.

Jaguar quality but reaches new heights with the XK8. The second thing I noticed was the reaction of other motorists. As I drove down the A45 dual-carriageway from the Browns Lane plant, being careful to observe the 60mph speed limit (not easy!), another car drew alongside, lingered and moved ahead. It pulled over and slowed down. I therefore overtook again, and also pulled over, at which point it came past again – and driver and passenger had a good look from their Mercedes-Benz!

I drove that night to Wales where the intention was to spend a couple of days photographing the Coupé. Mid-Wales was ideal not only as a backdrop with breathtaking scenery, but also for assessing the car. Welsh roads vary from fast, well-surfaced highways with sweeping bends, to lesser lanes with rough surfaces. A number of the roads I know well, which in my opinion helps enormously to judge a car. Above all, Welsh roads are so remarkably free of traffic.

It is challenging to say what impresses most about the XK8. It is so immediately obvious that the car is exceptional in every department. The performance is tremendous. The low first gear enables you to make a very rapid initial surge forward and the combination of the exceptional torque and four further gears ensure that this seriously exciting acceleration is maintained up to very high speeds. The Coupé takes just 6.5sec to 60mph (6.8sec to 100kph) and reaches a maximum of 156mph (251kph), yet achieves 23mpg (10.7 litres per 100km). These figures totally overshadow the competition.

You have the confidence to drive fast, when conditions allow, because the handling and brakes are on a par with the performance. The stability and predictability of the car just inspire so much trust. The combination of the Pirelli tyres and superbly developed suspension mean that you have to be very brutal to get the car to slide. When the back end does break away, you need your wits about you but the car does not catch you out.

A major contribution to confidence comes from the way the car rides over all manner of bumps, potholes and undulations without upsetting either its poise, or the comfort of the occupants. It absorbs the imperfections uncannily. In this respect and a number of others the XK8, not surprisingly, displays family resemblances. It shares youthful agility and superlative ride quality with the latest XJ saloons.

For a relatively large car, it turns into bends notably crisply, with a high level of grip and no sense of initial understeer. It is utterly neutral and tolerant of adjustment in mid-bend. I am told you can stamp on the brakes in

mid-corner without drama, and can well believe it.

The brakes are absolutely fantastic. Welsh sheep wander unfettered in many rural areas. While I like mutton, I like animals even more. Once or twice examples of less than intelligent Welsh sheep tested, or threatened to test, the XK8's brakes, which responded with massive assurance. With such awesome braking power, allied to delightful balance and feel, you can leave your braking very late and drive deep into bends.

In the past I have been less than enthusiastic about Jaguar's power steering. The steering on my 1973 XJ Coupé, for example, lacks feel and seems massively over-assisted. What a contrast! The clever combination of speed-sensitive assistance and variable ratio work a treat on the XK8. An enthusiastic driver receives the required messages at speed and yet the assistance is there for parking. The steering is an enormous step forward.

I would be lying if I said that I like automatic transmission, but clearly I am an oddity. There is only microscopic demand today for a manual gearbox on a car of this nature and it must be admitted that automatics are exceptionally good now. The gear changes are close to unnoticeable and the 'box is very responsive. The 'J' gate control allows second, third and fourth to be selected manually. For me the travel across the gate from the fully automatic mode, which includes the option of fifth, to manual operation is a little excessive, but I am being hyper-critical. Where the Jaguar scores over the competition is when cornering. An automatic transmission changing down mid-bend can be most disconcerting, but the XK8 senses it is being subjected to 'G' forces and inhibits any desire it may have to change gear.

The new V8 engine is clearly superlative. The automatic transmission does not allow you fully to realise just

Reach the open road and the XK8 is raring to go. It instantly inspires confidence, feeling both extremely quick and decidedly safe. The massive sub-woofer is trimmed in the parcel shelf colour on production models.

Jaguars have always been automotive art forms. Sir William Lyons knew the importance of style and the XK8 perpetuates his legacy.

how remarkably the torque is. The power, however, is memorable and the smooth refinement extraordinary. Make no mistake. This is a great engine. With 290bhp (216kW) on tap, and 290lb ft (393Nm) of torque, it is more powerful than the BMW 840 Ci (282bhp), Carrera 2 and 911 Porsches (282bhp), Lexus SC 400 (264bhp) and the Mercedes SL320 (228bhp). On the road the Lexus feels positively slow in comparison, but impressively refined. Yet the new Jaguar AJ-V8 engine matches that refinement while delivering 10% more power.

The body structure is clearly very torsionally stiff and the overall stability of the car, with its superlative straight-line, handling and braking abilities, really is stunning. But as with any Jaguar, the XK8 is schizophrenic, in

that it exhibits deeply polarised characters. This is, without question, a very fast and safe sports car, yet it is also a docile creature that is happy to potter around all day. Whichever way you wish to behave, the refinement is almost intrusive.

When city friends visit me in the country they say the silence hits them. It is the same with the XK. The sealing system, with the automatic window drop when you open a door, is exceptional. The noise, vibration and harshness levels are just so subdued. The winds in Wales were ferocious but the interior remained serene and the stability was unaffected.

The interior is traditional and tasteful. I like it. The seats hold you well and comfortably, without causing

any awkward movements when you climb in and out of the car. The massive veneered dashboard is positively decadent, like lashings of smoked salmon or Chateau Lascombes. I love it!

Actually it is the little details that particularly stick in the mind. The action of switching the heater fan control feels so good, as if it has been engineered with precision. The direction indicators emit a soothing sound akin to a metronome. The audio system selection and volume can be operated by the left thumb without the hand ever leaving the steering wheel. Similarly, the cruise control can be set, cancelled and resumed by the right thumb. Incidentally, I had previously only felt inclined to use cruise control in the USA before now, but found the logic of the controls in the XK8's installation took all the strain out of keeping religiously to, or very near to, speed limits. A couple of buttons permit the set speed to be incrementally increased or decreased, allowing delicate adjustment.

The heating and air conditioning controls are eminently sensible and utterly logical. You simply adjust the numerically displayed temperature required and the system does the rest. One morning I was up at an ungodly hour in the interests of dramatic photography and ice covered the car, but the windows cleared swiftly and the interior rapidly became hospitable.

The XK8 combines true style and excitement with genuine practicality. A boot, or trunk, is not a glamorous attribute, but it is very necessary if you are going to live with this car and use it. I thought that for a car of this type it was positively cavernous. My wife could not resist joining me for the trip; it swallowed our luggage, my work and her hats (she is the Imelda Marcos of hats) with ease.

Visibility is good. You cannot see the corners and it is quite a large car, but you soon get used to that. The front screen pillars are quite broad but again you adjust to that. I am desperately searching for something negative to say to prove my objectivity, but it is not easy. The best I can do is say that I found it a little difficult to read the main instruments, which are well recessed, something I actually like very much, when wearing sunglasses! But I

As with any Jaguar, the immediate sensation when you first drive an XK8 is one of great refinement and superlative ride. The car is very happy to be driven gently and is without temperament.

There are few joys to exceed the pleasure of open air motoring. The fully automatic, power-latching hood can be operated at speeds up to 10mph and takes around 20 seconds to complete its cycle. Production cars do not have the straight furrows seen on this prototype hood cover.

gather this car was not representative in that these instruments will be permanently illuminated on production cars. I would also prefer to have non-reflective glass for the minor instruments. End of criticisms!

When an early Convertible became available a few weeks later, I spent two days with it in nearby Shropshire. I have always loved open sports cars and own several. The XK8 Convertible transports the art form to new heights. The sophistication of the new power-latching soft-top is a revelation. Unlike its competitors, it is fully padded and insulated, negating the need for a hard-top in winter. With its heated rear window and superior sealing, the Convertible is so utterly practical, and yet the style is something else.

The weather was pretty appalling, with heavy rain at times, and yet with the soft-top up the refinement was superior to most saloons. It even hailed once when I had the soft-top down. My editor was driving my E-type in convoy and found it impossible to continue through the hail due to painful shotblasting on his face! But in the XK8 this assault from the weather did not trouble me at all. Similarly, showers did not inconvenience me provided I kept moving, and when the sun came out it was a positive joy to be motoring in the open air. Interestingly, my wife preferred the Convertible because she felt it was more of a sports car than the Coupé and, though the judgement is marginal, I think I agree.

I make no apologies for this being a eulogy. I am unashamedly overwhelmed by the awesome abilities of this remarkable sports car. As I have been the first to drive and write about these new classics, I cannot hide behind the collective view that will become established by a posse of road testers. I must make my own judgement in isolation.

I think the Jaguar XK8 will go down in history as a worthy successor to its great forebears, the XK120 and the E-type. Against its competitors of today, it will be judged pre-eminent.

If the mood takes you, the XK8 can be hurled around like a true sports car. The reserves of roadholding are massive, the handling neutral and forgiving.

THE XK8 HERITAGE

That the XK120 was not just a beauty was confirmed at Jabbeke in 1949 when this car achieved 132mph to establish the new Jaguar as the fastest production car in the world. Countless race and rally successes followed.

There is no question that the XK8 has a distinguished heritage. This chapter looks briefly at the Jaguar sports car lineage and the many still-born designs the company considered during the past three decades to succeed its great sports cars of the fifties and sixties.

This sports car story began in 1935 with the SS Jaguar 100, a new saloon-related model from SS Cars Ltd that adopted the new Jaguar name. Jaguar's founder, William Lyons, designed a beautiful and rakish body to clothe the conventional chassis and engines manufactured by the Standard Motor Company. Produced with 2½-litre and later 3½-litre engines, these cars were lively performers due to their light weight and good torquey engines. Indeed the '3½' is a revelation even today and can be hustled along twisting country roads with verve.

Apart from being the starting point for Jaguar's genuine sports cars, as opposed to its other sporting saloons, the SS 100 illustrated two fundamentals. Firstly, Lyons was a brilliant automotive designer who knew the value of style. He realised that style sold motor cars, and indeed it could be argued that the other SS and SS Jaguar models appealed only for their style because performance did not match the promise of their extravagantly sporty coachwork. Secondly, the company still relied on another supplier for its engines, although it had progressed a long way from its origins as a manufacturer of motorcycle sidecars and coachbuilt Austin Sevens. The Standard engines were solid, reliable workhorses, neither innovative nor exciting.

Admittedly the distinguished and irascible engineer, Harry Weslake, had worked some magic upon these engines by redesigning the valve gear, but SS needed its own engine if the company was to be taken seriously. This was an essential element in the image of a proper motor company – and Lyons was an ambitious man.

The young but growing company took a big step forward in 1935 with the appointment of William Heynes as Chief Engineer, and the small engineering team was further strengthened in 1938 when the great Walter Hassan joined. These two, together with Claude Baily, were given the task during the war years of designing a suitable engine.

The result was the XK power unit. Cliché though it is, the engine was to become legendary. It was innovative, having twin overhead camshafts. With its superb polished cam covers, it had the visual glamour that was an important part of the design brief. In 3.4-litre production form it delivered superb power and torque, and proved to have great development potential. It was ready for production three years after the war ended.

Jaguar, as the company was now named, had no sports car in production immediately after the war, but such a car would be good for the company's image, providing excitement and competition potential. Although the XK engine was intended primarily for the more important saloon car range that was being developed, and in particular an all-new large saloon, Jaguar decided that the new power unit could usefully be proven in advance of its appearance in a saloon if the company

made a few sports cars – say a couple of hundred – that would be bought by a rather more tolerant crowd of enthusiast owners.

The decision was made to produce a sports car in time for the London Motor Show in October 1948. With only weeks to go, Lyons designed a body of stunning and lasting beauty, and Heynes produced a cut-down version of his latest chassis. A prototype 3.2-litre XK engine was inserted in this hand-crafted body and the car was revealed to the public, although it had never run!

The XK120, the 120 standing for its hoped-for maximum speed, stole the show. As we all know now, the car was a sensation. It brought racing car performance to the road, yet was docile and easy to drive. The car had good roadholding but was comfortable and refined for a sports car. It was to prove utterly reliable and the price was unbelievably low. But above all, it was endowed with a body of great beauty.

In 1951 a Fixed Head Coupé version of the basic Roadster was added, its body style both captivating and inspirational. A third XK120 variant, the Drophead Coupé, arrived in 1953.

Demand for the XK120 far outstripped the most optimistic estimates and the new sports car led Jaguar's, and Britain's, vital post-war export drive in America. The XK120 proved to be officially the fastest production car in the world and proceeded to win countless races and rallies. An exploratory and rather half-hearted foray to the Le Mans 24 Hours in 1950 very nearly resulted in a top-three finish against thinly disguised racing machines. This one race was of particular significance because it was not only known throughout Europe, but its fame in the USA was second only to that of the Indianapolis 500. It made the front pages of the newspapers, and Lyons knew this.

Bill Heynes and Service Manager 'Lofty' England persuaded Lyons that Jaguar could win Le Mans if it could design a car using the XK engine and certain other production components, but with a lighter chassis and a more aerodynamic body. Malcolm Sayer, an aerodynamicist, joined the team and three XK120Cs (or C-types as they would become known, the 'C' standing for competition) were built just in time for the 1951 race. A young Stirling Moss, who had already boosted his growing reputation with a brilliant win in the 1950 Tourist Trophy race in an XK120, was signed up to lead the team.

Moss set a searing pace at Le Mans in 1951 but retired with a minor fault, as did the second car. The third, piloted by Peter Walker and Peter Whitehead, took a famous victory and put Jaguar on the map world-wide.

A second win followed in 1953, the year the Queen was crowned and Hillary conquered Everest, when Duncan Hamilton and Tony Rolt beat most of the top

In 1954 the XK120 was succeeded by the XK140, which refined the concept and benefited from better steering, brakes and legroom, and a more powerful engine. The Drophead Coupé (seen here) and Fixed Head Coupé versions also had small rear seats.

The D-type was both highly successful and brilliantly innovative. The pioneering two-seater aluminium monocoque was surmounted by Malcolm Sayer's superb body design, which would influence the XK8 style some 40 years later.

Grand Prix drivers and virtually all the famous teams to set the first ever 100mph average for the endurance classic. Their triumph was due in no small part to the disc brakes that Jaguar had developed with Dunlop.

In 1954 the XK120 was succeeded by the XK140, again available in Roadster, Fixed Head Coupé and Drophead Coupé versions, and the D-type also replaced the C-type. Like the XK120s, most XK140s were exported and comparatively few remained in Britain. As for the D-type, it is quite simply most enthusiasts' idea of the classic fifties sports racing car. Highly innovative with monocoque construction, dry-sump lubrication, alloy wheels, rubber bag fuel tanks, disc brakes and, later, fuel injection, the D-type has often been called an aircraft on wheels, with good reason. The body was once again the work of Sayer and contributed greatly to the car's performance against the more powerful Ferraris. The sheer, sculptural beauty was a complete coincidence – the D-type was designed for efficiency.

After being delayed early on by fine grit in their fuel at Le Mans in 1954, the D-type of Hamilton and Rolt failed to beat the winning Ferrari by just 105 seconds after 24 hours of hard racing in atrocious conditions. Victories followed, however, in 1955, 1956 and 1957, D-types finishing 1-2-3-4-6 in the final year. When Moss departed to Mercedes-Benz in 1955 to further his Grand Prix career, Mike Hawthorn replaced him as team leader.

Following the awful Le Mans accident in 1955, it was assumed that engine size would be restricted. Jaguar began developing a car that ultimately became the E-type, or XK-E as it was always known in the USA. Evolved directly from the D-type and launched in 1961, the fabulous E-type was as great a sensation as the XK120 had been in 1948, and once again set new standards for sports cars.

Powered by a three-carburettor version of the XK engine, the E-type had a top speed of around 150mph yet, in true Jaguar tradition, was docile and flexible. Indeed refinement was exceptional for a car of this type and the price, half the cost of comparable Ferraris and Aston Martins, was once again difficult to believe. Fitted with new independent rear suspension developed by Bob Knight (who would later succeed Heynes), the E-type was endowed with both a uniquely sophisticated ride for a sports car, and excellent, predictable handling.

A car's true ability is often proven, or exposed, on the race track. The brand new E-type won its very first race in the hands of Graham Hill against Ferrari and Aston Martin opposition. It was the first of a vast number of successes around the world.

The E-type is remembered, and treasured, as an exciting performance car, but of course it had something more – it had style. The early cars, with their clean simplicity and sensual beauty, were once again works of sculpture by Malcolm Sayer. This extraordinary man used a long-hand version of what is today called Computer Aided Design (CAD) and claimed the E-type was the first production car to be designed mathematically. He hated, incidentally, to be called a stylist. However, the style, which was watered down a little in later versions, was brilliant, whether in open Roadster or closed Fixed Head Coupé guises.

The E-type had enormous influence on the XK8, but a great deal more happened, or did not happen, in the intervening decades before Jaguar once again followed the path of great, innovative engineering and sensational style.

Opinions differ about the V12-engined Series III E-type, the last of the E-type line. The car looked heavier, suffered from a surfeit of chrome and, with power steering, was a very different animal from the 3.8 and Series I 4.2 E-types. The new 5.3-litre V12 engine, introduced in 1971, was undoubtedly superb, but it only served to heighten the realisation that the great E-type was ageing. With Jaguar now a part of the gargantuan British Leyland fiasco, quality was poor and sales in the all-important US market died away, in spite of a racing programme with Group 44 on the East Coast and Huffaker Racing on the West Coast.

Jaguar management had been grappling for some time with the problem of whether to develop the E-type or replace it, and if so with what. In fact, these deliberations can be traced right back to the very earliest days of the E-type. Even as it was being launched in New York, a couple of weeks after its debut at Geneva, Lyons telephoned the factory in Coventry to say that he wanted a larger car. Not surprisingly, the Americans had expressed reservations about the cabin size, and legroom in particular.

"I want more room in the car: I shall be back at the weekend and I want to see one," Lyons is reputed to have said. While Lyons wanted a longer car, Heynes argued for a wider one and, at one point, put forward a suggestion that Jaguar should build a Ford Thunderbird competitor. There was also concern that the E-type was too long for Europe and versions were drawn with shorter bonnets. They looked truly appalling!

Lyons was undoubtedly a styling genius but he was an autocratic man who was not close even to his senior men, as former PR chief Bob Berry recalls: "Bill Heynes had to make his mechanical bits fit the Lyons bodyshells.

The E-type translated many features first seen on the racing C-types and D-types into a stunning production car. This early prototype, without chromed headlamp rims, is seen at MIRA with Chief Tester Norman Dewis.

This prototype Fixed Head E-type, registered 9600 HP, became the press car and established the 150mph legend.

In 1971 the superb V12 engine was launched in the E-type, which as a result became more 'grand touring' than 'sports' in character. Clever photography here disguises the ugly US bumper appendages...

In the mid-sixties Jaguar looked at a number of possibilities to replace or supplement the E-type. There were thoughts of attacking the Ford Thunderbird market with a larger version, and from this proposal came the XJ6 saloon, launched in 1968.

Situations arose where Sir William was busy forging ahead with his body styling and Bill was trying to interpret what was going on both in terms of what the shape required, plus engineering the mechanical side."

Apart from copious drawings, some mock-ups were built and from one of these came the styling for the XJ6 saloon. The XJ6 rear body style was achieved by cutting off the last foot of the E-type tail. Another new avenue was explored in the mid-sixties when Heynes, who had been pushing Lyons for permission to build a sports racing car, was given the go-ahead and the fabulous mid-engined XJ13 was the result. Many feel it was Sayer's finest masterpiece. Thought was then given to a mid-engined road car and several models were made. Jim Randle, who would later succeed Heynes and Knight, remembers this concept as "totally impractical" and it went no further.

After many E-type variations had been considered, the 2+2 model was introduced in 1966. The same year Lyons sold out to BMC, which already had a large sports car range, and the organisation became known as British Motor Holdings (BMH). The plan then was to supersede the Austin-Healey 3000 – a sports car from the BMC fold – with two new Austin-Healey models in 1968, a '4000' with a Rolls-Royce engine in the spring and a GT 2+2 with a 3-litre XK engine in the autumn.

Around this time a new project was begun within Jaguar and given the designation XJ21. This changed considerably in concept as it progressed, beginning with

E-type styling and then moving away in 1968 to new themes for both open and closed versions, the latter influenced by contemporary Italian styling, particularly the Pirana 'dream car' commissioned from Bertone by *The Daily Telegraph* and built upon a 2+2 E-type. This same year BMH became part of the newly formed and ultimately disastrous British Leyland empire.

Meanwhile, Heynes suggested that the V12 engine, which was soon to be ready, should be introduced in the E-type pro tem, until the all-new XJ21 was ready. In fact the British Leyland débâcle delayed the introduction of the V12 until 1971. The XJ21, for which the body tooling was about to be ordered, was then cancelled because another project had overtaken it.

On 9 September 1968, Malcolm Sayer sent a memo to Sir William Lyons suggesting a completely new concept, which would become the XJS. He proposed a "2+2 sports based on XJ4 parts". Confusingly, XJ4 was the internal codename for the XJ6! "The image sought after," wrote Sayer, "is of a low wide high speed car at least as eye-catching as those the Italians will produce, even if it means sacrificing some of the more sensible values such as luggage and passenger space, silence, ease of entry."

The delays and new US safety laws, actual and perceived, played a part in the decision, but there was another consideration as Oliver Winterbottom, who was then working in the Styling Department, explains. "The brief was that it was a sports-bodied XJ4 platform. We couldn't afford a brand new car – in fact we had gone

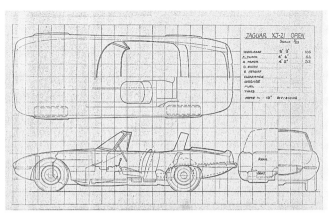

The XJ21, which was to be an E-type replacement, was drawn by Sayer in 1968 and very nearly went into production. It is fascinating to compare this design with the later Pininfarina Spyder and the XK8. Note this early appearance of XJS-style rear lights.

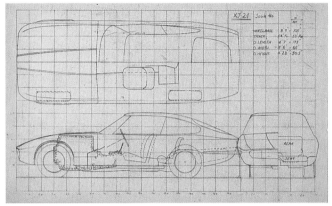

Malcolm Sayer designed several versions of an XJ21 Coupé, a model that showed an increasing Italian influence, most notably from the Pirana. This proposal features the distinctive Jaguar 'D' light (or rear quarterlight) that has been a hallmark of Jaguar sports cars for many years and has carried through to the XK8.

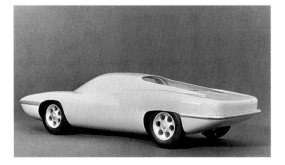

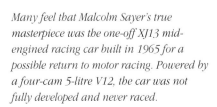

Many feel that Malcolm Sayer's true masterpiece was the one-off XJ13 mid-engined racing car built in 1965 for a possible return to motor racing. Powered by a four-cam 5-litre V12, the car was not fully developed and never raced.

Top right: The Pirana was a 'dream car' designed by the Italian styling house of Bertone for The Daily Telegraph and built on the floorpan of a 2+2 E-type with widened track and Dunlop racing tyres.

Above: There were ideas for a production version of the mid-engined XJ13 racing project. Three different scale models were made, including an open version, but were not progressed. The beginnings can be seen of the XJS's flying buttresses, as they have become known – they work on this car but did not happily transpose to the XJS.

into BMH because we couldn't afford the development of the XJ6. So the last thing anybody was going to be doing was developing totally new cars. I got involved in an alternative which was the XJ4GT."

While cost dictated that the new sports car had to be based on the saloon platform, the dreaded US regulations largely decreed and constrained the styling, as Bob Berry confirms. "The North American influence in the context of safety legislation was the guiding factor."

In fact, with the benefit of hindsight, we now know that fears of a US ban on open cars were unfounded, but a generation of sports cars was lost. Together with his outline suggestions for the new model, Sayer penned a number of drawings of possible body styles, including fastback and targa versions. The least attractive was chosen for production...

As to a name for the new sporting car, there was pressure to call it the F-type, as there had been when the V12 E-type was conceived. Bob Berry, who had been with Jaguar during the great days of the fifties and sixties, would have none of it and put his case to the man who was briefly Chief Executive. "I managed to persuade Geoffrey Robinson that it should not be called an F-type because it bore no relation to the E-type, and since it was a development of the XJ series we ought to call it XJS, standing for XJ Special."

No one could deny that the XJS was technically excellent, but it committed one cardinal sin, especially for a Jaguar. It lacked great beauty. Compare it with the XK120 and the E-type – Jaguar threw away all of its wonderful styling heritage. It may have been a factor that by this time Lyons was of advancing years and Sayer was not a fit man – he died in 1970 at the age of only 53.

The last E-types rolled off the production line in 1973 and after a brief hiatus the XJS appeared in 1975. The reception was a rather

For reasons of cost, the idea of basing a new sporting car on the XJ6 platform was explored. Several versions were considered, including this 'XJ4GT' proposed by the Styling Department.

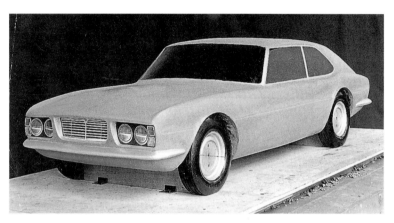

Malcolm Sayer produced many drawings for the new saloon-based sporting car and, without exception, they appear more pleasing than the finished XJS.

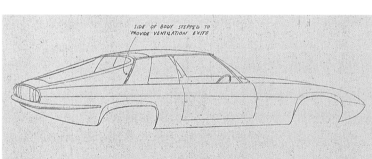

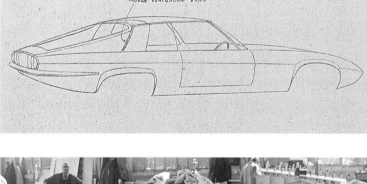

This early version of the eventual XJS shows many of the production features beginning to emerge. Note the V12 badge on the grille, and in the background what appears to be an XJ21. The number plate, which would date the car to 1965, appears to have been fitted to confuse historians!

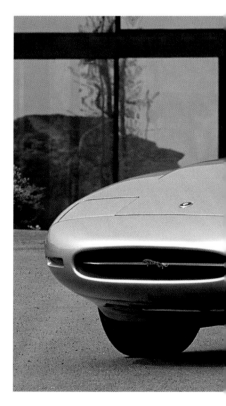

The XJS finally succeeded the E-type in 1975 and continued the transition from sports car to GT. Uniquely for a Jaguar, the styling was not universally acclaimed and many felt Jaguar had lost its way.

embarrassed silence. This was unprecedented for a Jaguar. I remember the day well, and I remember the great disappointment.

Three years later Pininfarina displayed an XJS Spyder styling exercise at the NEC Motor Show and many felt that, in an ideal world, this was the car Jaguar should have built. The message was not lost on Jaguar management when thoughts turned at the end of the decade to a

family of sports cars based on the forthcoming XJ40 saloon, which would be launched in 1986.

Once again it was a difficult time for Jaguar. The company's parent, British Leyland, had been nationalised and, following the Ryder Report commissioned by Anthony Wedgwood Benn, was implementing a policy of blind centralisation. This process included submerging the identity of Jaguar in a way that could only be inter-

The fabulous XJS-based Spyder was styled by Pininfarina and revealed at the 1978 NEC Motor Show. To many it was the car Jaguar should have built and, had funds been available, it is likely this styling exercise would have been adopted. However, the influence of this car, which coincidentally followed Sayer's XJ21 thinking, would become apparent.

preted as jealousy. The cost in financial terms was catastrophic and near fatal for Jaguar, as Bob Knight told me some years ago.

"Between 1968 and 1974 Jaguar had contributed £24 million positive cash flow – a lot of money at that time. That was in effect bullion that was hauled over the gate at Browns Lane and poured down the bottomless pit at Longbridge. This money could have made all the difference to Jaguar." There is no doubt that Knight, with his great intellect and outstanding engineering skills, saved Jaguar from complete extermination.

The XJ41 was to have been a high-performance sports car based on the XJ40 saloon. Martin Broomer, though tall, demonstrates that the car was very low indeed and may not have been totally feasible. Photographs of XJ41 have never before been released by Jaguar.

The new sporting car that was to be based on the XJ40 saloon was coded XJ41. Its birth and secret life were rather convoluted. Paul Walker, who is today Chief Engineer, Vehicle and Chassis Engineering, told me the story.

"XJ41 started out really as a means of getting BL Cars board approval, under Sir Michael Edwardes, for the XJ40. The concept at the time had been to spin off a sports car from the XJ40 floorpan, as with the XJS from the XJ6, by shortening the rear of the platform and moving the front wheel centre line forward relative to the engine, but otherwise keeping the XJ40 floorpan and suspensions unchanged. From that original desire, XJ41 then developed on and on, had features added, became heavier and more complex, and gained a twin-turbocharged engine. The power output then meant that we felt we needed to look at four-wheel drive, and the brakes were beefed up to cope with the extra speed. The price, both the tooling and 'piece' price, went up. The commonality with XJ40 diminished.

"XJ41 was carried out as a very 'stand-alone' programme, with a group of very bright, young but totally inexperienced engineers doing it as a completely CAD-driven project, with no older experience to help guide them the right way. So I think they worked naïvely, but with all the right intent.

"They felt they could throw features at the car and, of course, it would have sold because it was a sporting Jaguar. But they didn't really have the ability to look at the affordable business structure of what they were doing. The teams in Sales & Marketing and Engineering never really agreed about exactly what the XJ41 project was trying to be.

"In those days we were split in Engineering between Design and Development. So a group of guys in Design would draw a car. Development would build some prototypes and then say, 'Oh, these are no good'. Development would do the testing and make a judgement saying, 'Well this doesn't work, this is no good'.

They would raise a formal company problem report, a PRAR [Problem Report Action Request], on Design, obviously some months after the car had been drawn by someone who was now probably working on some other component, or another project. Then the designer would do a revision and the project would go through the whole loop again. All the communication between the Design and Development groups was really through the hardware, and a problem-reporting – 'I don't like what you've done' – process.

"The organisational structure went right up to Rex Marvin on Development and Tom Jones on Design, and they worked for Jim Randle. So that was the first point at which Design and Development came together. So the whole structure of the way we worked was not destined to give the best results."

As Director of Sales & Marketing, Roger Putnam had strong views on the XJ41, and its convertible sister, the

XJ42. "Although the XJS was before my time at Jaguar, it was never seen as a competent successor to E-type, in terms of creating the excitement or perhaps having the breadth of appeal. Having said that, the XJS acquitted itself extraordinarily well as a different type of sports car, a grand touring car.

"When I first joined Jaguar in 1982, John Egan was, at that stage, trying to pull the company out of BL. The successor to the XJS, or indeed the E-type, was already in clay at the bottom end of the factory. I wasn't actively involved in styling committees at that time, although I was shown the car very early on and asked for my opinion of it. It was a lot slimmer, narrower, less sporty and macho than it finished up in later days.

"Over the next five or six years, the car seemed to make little progress but eventually, towards the end of the eighties, Sales & Marketing were finally allowed to drive some of the prototypes. My initial reaction was one of huge disappointment. The car was over-weight and over-priced, and it under-performed. At about that time Ford acquired the company and I was asked by John Grant, on behalf of the Ford management, for my candid views on the car. I said pretty much what I thought.

"I think my view was echoed by many of the non-engineering senior management, and the upshot was that

Ford was unable to see a way to make this car actually work without immense additional investment. So we then opened up a debate about where we should take the model range. At that time a wholly new successor to XJ40, called XJ90, was being planned. Having scrapped XJ41 and XJ42, simply because it was impossible to reconcile design specification and market requirements, we had to do a complete review of what Ford's cheque book would stretch to.

"The outcome so far has been extremely successful. Having redesigned the XJ40 and changed it fundamentally in character, we have a success on our hands in the X300 saloon. We also looked at some facelifted XJSs.

"Whether I was the one who put the wooden stake through XJ41, I shall never know!"

As well as showing how not to develop a new car, the unfortunate saga of XJ41 serves to illustrate how dramatically Jaguar has changed in the nineties. Jaguar's failings were in its organisational structure, not in its undoubted engineering capability. Ford's benign influence since it purchased Jaguar in 1989 has harnessed and disciplined the raw ability.

The story of the XK8, therefore, is more than the story of a great car, a really worthy successor to the XKs and E-types. It is also the story of the revival of Jaguar.

The XJ41 was unquestionably influenced by the Pininfarina Spyder and there are some similarities with the XK8 (seen in the background), but these extend only to the styling. Beneath the skin, the XK8 is another story.

THE EARLY UPS AND DOWNS OF X100 – 1991-92

The styling process began in 1991 with thoughts of re-skinning the XJS. However, the XJS has a 'knee-cracker' door and Manufacturing was keen to dispense with this as it caused quality problems. It was realised that if the front wing was re-tooled, the whole car may as well be re-designed.

The rebirth of Jaguar began with the Ford acquisition in 1989. Jaguar's fortunes during that decade had fluctuated enormously, and generally in line with the ever mercurial dollar/sterling relationship. In broad terms, every cent made a difference of £3 million a year to Jaguar's bottom line. Thus the company's financial performance ranged from the heights of success to the depths of despair.

As with any business, healthy profits were vital for Jaguar to generate the funds to invest in new facilities, top-flight personnel and, above all, new products. Quality had sunk to an all-time low during the nationalised BL era, but efforts had been made to improve the situation following privatisation in 1984. In reality, quality did not improve sufficiently and the claims began to wear thin. A return to sports car racing with TWR helped to maintain a good image, which received another boost at the end of the decade with the XJ220 supercar.

However, with an adverse currency situation and falling US demand, Jaguar's finances were rapidly deteriorating. Ford had actually been courting Jaguar for a couple of years and its advances had been roundly rebuffed. By 1989, however, Jaguar had to face reality. GM entered the frame until Ford delivered a knockout punch in the form of an offer of £1600 million. For that sum, Ford bought £300 million of antiquated assets, but, more importantly, a fantastic name and a presence in the luxury car sector.

The X100 (as the XK8 was codenamed internally) styling process began with a series of sketch proposals in which all manner of different ideas and concepts were explored. The stylists were encouraged to be both traditional and radical.

This early sketch shows how an XJS-derived car might have looked, with frontal treatment evocative of the X300 saloon that had been styled by this time but would not be launched until 1994.

It would have been ironic if the sports car rear had been influenced by XJ saloon styling because, as we have seen, that theme was itself derived from the E-type. This proposal has the feeling more of a coupé version of the saloon rather than a new sports car.

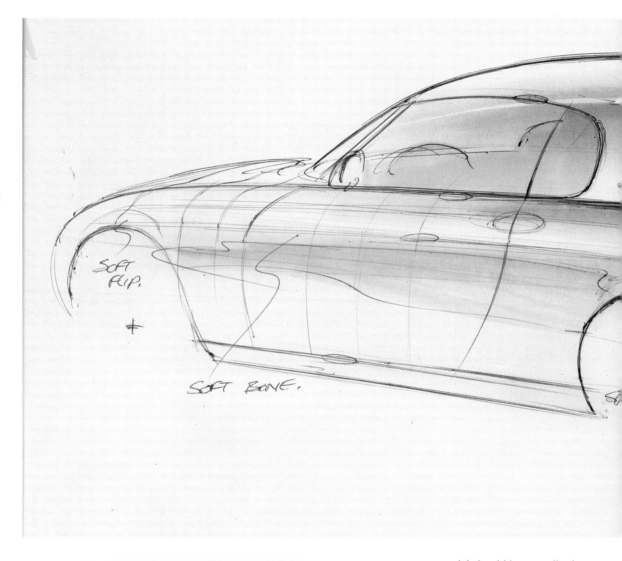

Here the stylist has noted features that needed refinement or change. This is a typical development sketch that illustrates the way a design gradually moves towards the production reality.

Although it is very much more sporty, this car still has something of the feel of the XJS at the front. There are certainly no E-type cues as yet, but interestingly the familiar Jaguar 'D' light rear side window appears in all the sketches. Stylists love to exaggerate wheels and tyres!

As described in the previous chapter, an early decision was to scrap the XJ41 – or F-type as it was often known outside the company – and write off the £15 million that had been invested in the project. The totally revamped XJ saloon to replace the XJ40 range was already under way and would be known internally as the X300. A debate then took place as to whether the next new model should be a small saloon or a replacement for the XJS. As for the latter, a project had already started with a team run by Martin Broomer, who was then Manager of the Sports Car Programme Office under Chris Colombo.

Traditionally the USA has been Jaguar's most important market and this remains true today. In early post-war Britain companies could only obtain steel if they exported a high proportion of their products – 'Export Or Die' was the dictum by which the British Government encouraged industry to regenerate and rebuild. Jaguar had little choice but to cultivate the vast US market.

The XK120 led that crusade, both for the company and the country. Hollywood embraced the 120 and many film stars acquired examples. The larger saloons, or sedans as they are known in the US, and the later 'compact' saloons benefited from the excitement created by

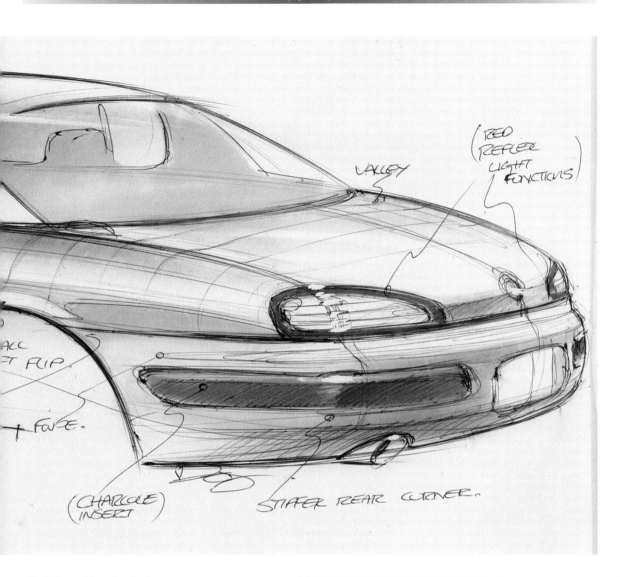

VALLEY

(RED REFLER LIGHT FUNCTIONS)

ACC FLIP.

FORE.

(CHARCOLE) INSERT

STIFFER REAR CORNER.

the XKs, and later by the E-types.

Mike Dale, an expatriate Brit based in the US, moved from British Leyland to Jaguar when the latter extricated itself. After some years as a Vice President of Jaguar Cars Inc, he became President of the company in 1990.

"The success we had in the eighties with the sedan," states Dale, "is the only time that Jaguar in the US, or Canada, has ever succeeded with a sedan. Jaguar was a sports car. That's what it was known as, that's what Clark Gable owned. The sedan was a great commercial success and seen as probably the most elegant sedan in the marketplace in the eighties, but sports cars have always been the soul of Jaguar. The odd thing is that while the XJS has been far more successful commercially, having sold 115,000 world-wide and having been far more successful in the US than the E-type in numbers, it never grasped people's imaginations the same way.

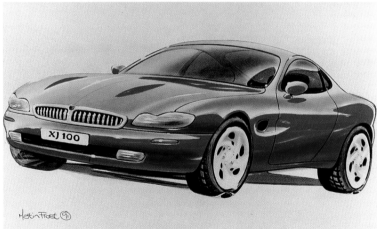

"As we've recovered in the nineties, the X300, particularly the long-wheelbase version, has re-established the base of Jaguar in the US. The necessity for the new sports car, even though its volume is going to be much lower, is that it rejuvenates the soul of Jaguar.

"That's absolutely vital when you're selling a prestige vehicle, because in the end you sell prestige vehicles

The Jaguar 'D' light first appeared on the Mark V saloon in 1950. The tradition was strengthened with the XK Fixed Heads, the Mark II saloons and the E-type, but significantly the XJS lacked this strong Jaguar identity. A distinctive front grille would make a comeback on cars of all types by the mid-nineties.

Dated February 1992, this sketch of a possible tail style gives strong XK8 clues. The theme would eventually re-emerge towards the end of the year.

This contentious proposal might not have appealed to the traditional XJS owner, but pushing the limits was an important part of the styling process.

through emotion. Certainly you must have competitive specifications, prices and quality, but these things amount to the starting line for the race. If you want to excel in the race, you must have the legends, as we have with Le Mans and in our racing in the States over the last 20 years. The spiritual side of any marque is absolutely essential, and that's why XJ41 was vital to the success of the company. It was also vital, once XJ41 was no longer part of the product plan, to replace it with something more than the XJS.

"For the past 30 years the passion of our customers and of the people who run the company has defied the often uneven supply, uncompetitive specifications and poor quality. The passion has made people hang on and keep the company alive. Mercedes-Benz owners say – and you see this in the research all the time – they like their cars, and so they should, they're fine automobiles. But Jaguar owners say they love theirs.

"I'll give you an example of how people get sucked into Jaguar. Clive Ennos had been a Ford man all his life. I would say that within a year, Clive lived and breathed Jaguar. It's wonderful to see it."

Clive Ennos arrived at Jaguar in 1990, having received what he describes as "a wonderful offer to join Jaguar to develop a vehicle and component engineering group". Indeed he had always had a love of Jaguars. "I think that is something most British engineers are born with." As Director, Product Engineering Operations, he is now in charge of Engineering within Jaguar.

"I've seen many changes here," says Ennos. "When the dollar was close to parity, Jaguar was making quite a lot of money. John Egan decided to build a good engineering centre and bought Whitley. A lot of engineering people were recruited, and the numbers rose from 300-400 to 1050 by the time I arrived. Most of these people hadn't delivered a product because there hadn't been

Four clay models were created early in 1992 to develop the themes that had been established. The brief for Clay 1, by Ghia of Turin, part of Ford, was to design a traditional luxury GT car. As the customer base was existing XJS owners, the thinking went, it might make sense to build an evolutionary car to satisfy them. Clay 1 did not proceed beyond the second styling review that took place in June 1992.

Clay 3 was XJS-derived and styled by Ford at Dearborn to a brief from Jaguar. This split clay, offering two variations on a 'progressive' theme, has a few cues from Jaguar's past: the slender bumpers are a link to the E-type and the grille alternatives are reminiscent of XKs and Mark II saloons. The XJS derivation, however, meant that this shape had no haunches and no curving 'D' light. Clay 3 was considered to be too close to the XJS and dropped out of the picture in March 1992.

Clay 2, which was created at Whitley, was intended to pursue a radical theme, to be avant-garde and to test the water. It was a conscious attempt to break away from Jaguar tradition.

it successfully, and it really was a major step forward, we went from literally no timing controls to World Class Timing, without passing go.

"Within Ford, you would have another goal each year to improve on timing, but we had to make a quantum leap from releasing things literally when somebody thought they were ready" – Ennos delivers a hearty peal of laughter – "as opposed to releasing them when you said you were going to and when the market actually needed you to.

"After X300, the replacement for the XJS was the next most urgent project. It was an incredible car – out there for 20 years. The heritage is wonderful, but it did need to be updated. So we had a very interesting time because Ford was still trying to find out what it had bought. They really didn't know fully. Until X300 had been launched successfully, the question in their minds was, 'Can these guys actually do it? They are unproven.' The word unproven was used several times. I went to the meetings and they'd say, 'I know you keep telling me they're well qualified and they're young, but they're unproven.'

"It was actually true. There were some exceptional people, like Trevor Crisp, who has been with the company for 40 years and is probably the best engine man in the country. There were several people like that around and thank goodness. And then there were the young up-and-coming guys, like Dave Szczupak in the Engine Group. They could learn from the really experienced people and build from that. Being a small manufacturer, which is the one advantage Jaguar has, meant this worked very well. We're all on one site, whereas when I was with Ford I was spending most of my time sitting in an aeroplane."

The word 'chimney' is regularly used by Jaguar personnel to describe one aspect of the company's organisation in the past. By this they mean a separate, seemingly autonomous area of the company that appeared to have little communication or co-operation with other areas.

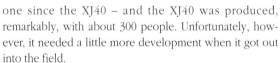

one since the XJ40 – and the XJ40 was produced, remarkably, with about 300 people. Unfortunately, however, it needed a little more development when it got out into the field.

"There was no really affordable and containable cycle plan at that stage. Once a cycle plan had been put together, we had a superb talent base here in the engineering group. It's a very young group and the average age, when I arrived, was only just over 30. Even now it's only about 34/35, in spite of my great age pulling it up. That was excellent in that we were very open-minded and could take on board some of the Ford processes and disciplines, and use them to really excellent effect.

"So the X300 was the first programme on which we pulled together. Having gone through that and launched

Like many styling exercises, Clay 2 became less adventurous as it progressed, but it is considered preferable to start with a wild design and tame it rather than warm up a staid concept. Clay 2 was an attempt to explode the myth that the Jaguar styling department is good at approaching design from an evolutionary perspective but not at breaking frontiers. Radical though it was, Clay 2 did at least have a grille reminiscent of the C-type sports racing car.

"There were enormous chimneys when I arrived," continues Ennos. "Whitley used to be called 'the bunker'. I asked Roger Putnam why, and he said, 'because every now and again – not very often – this lid would open and a car would pop out, and then the lid would close, and then Manufacturing would pick it up, take it in and try to build it, and then they'd give it to us to sell it.'

These were all independent actions. So you'd build great prototypes!

"Over the past five or six years this has changed out of all recognition. We're not called 'the bunker' any more, although 'the garden centre' became another nickname because of the plants and open spaces! But we really do work closely together now. I know if I have a problem I can pick up the 'phone up to Mike Beasley, the Manufacturing Director, and if he can help he will. All my Chief Engineers have this sort of close relationship with David Hudson who runs the plants, and it works extremely well."

In late 1991, the decision was taken to initiate a project for a replacement XJS, with the product planning co-ordinated by Martin Broomer, Manager of the Sports Car Programme Office. Martin describes how the process begins.

"Our role was to establish the product vision for the new car and to define the objectives, working with the key functions – Sales & Marketing, Engineering and Finance. We looked at a range of concepts and presented our findings and recommendations to the Product Committee. Given the company's parlous financial position at the time, the decision process became fairly protracted as we wrestled with the alternatives, trying to establish a viable and

Clay 2 actually made it through the March and June reviews, and was down to the last two entering the July review – where it fell by the wayside. By this stage feasibility and legislative requirements had somewhat sanitised the design: note the larger lamps and apertures, the reworking of the sills to a more rounded shape, and similar changes to the lower areas at front and rear.

affordable business case that would satisfy the Jaguar and Ford Boards."

Paul Stokes, Purchasing Director, describes how the process develops.

"At different times, different people hold the same ball. It starts with the Product Committee, which decides that it's going to build a car. 'What is this car to be, Sales & Marketing? What do you want?' You pass the stick and it's their turn to lead. Very shortly after that they begin working with Engineering, who start to look towards us in Purchasing and ask, 'Which suppliers are we likely to be using? What's our strategy with air conditioning systems, for instance?' And so it develops."

"The evolution," recalls Mike Dale, "really started from a marketing point of view by us asking what we could do with the XJS to refresh it. You have to view this in the context of what was happening at the time. As we went through that process, we realised that Jaguar in the future was going to be so much more than anything we had dreamt it could be. This was more than the renaissance of Jaguar. This was forging a new Jaguar, on an old base, that had the potential to achieve far more."

At around this time, Manfred Lampe joined Jaguar. He was instrumental in the development of many process improvements and new technologies within Engineering and Styling. As a result of these improve-

ments, the small Jaguar styling team was able to take on the enormous task of developing several clay models concurrently within a severely compressed time scale.

"Manfred did something very interesting," continues Mike Dale. "While we were scratching our heads about the styling of this thing, he went back into what has been written about Jaguars by people like you over the

make a new car out of it. We looked at that for several weeks, and had many presentations, both internally and with Ford. We needed to alter the car sufficiently to justify that sort of money. But we couldn't make it work. There was simply too much XJS coming through and the feeling was that it would be foolish to launch a car with a new engine but with a body that resembled the last

past 50 years, and particularly about the Jaguars that we admired – 120s, 140s, E-types. What did you say? What were the adjectives? What adjectives were used for the cars we didn't like? We just sat there, the Styling Committee, discussing how to make people write those things again. So much of this is a matter of the heart, of emotion."

Fergus Pollock is based in Styling and would later become Design Manager for the project that was given the internal designation X100.

"We were asked initially to look at a £99 million facelift to the XJS. So we were asked to carry over the cabin and the doors, but to change the nose and tail – to

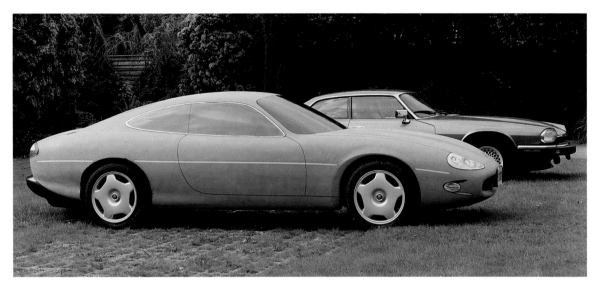

With the 'evocative' theme established as the way to progress, it was felt that a further alternative was needed – so Clay A was created. It benefited enormously from being shortened and even in bare clay looked the part – subtle XJ220 influences can be discerned in the rear sill treatment and upswept rear bumper.

model, especially when you consider that the age group of Jaguar buyers was getting older and older. That's something you have to watch, because it indicates you're not making enough conquest sales.

"So the £99 million slug got increased and we were looking at effectively an all-new car, but one based upon certain hard points. Towards the end of 1991 we elected to examine four different strategies so that management had a choice. Submitting one design isn't good enough – you have to work your way through a range of alternatives."

Although the idea of a further XJS facelift was abandoned and the whole project was scaled up very considerably as a consequence, it was decreed that the new car must still be based on the XJS floorpan.

"Because we were coming off an 'S'," continues Pollock, "and because our customer base was 'S' and we wanted to maintain that and build upon it, we looked at a traditional 'S'-derived theme, an 'evolutionary' car – this became Clay 1. The next theme was 'evocative' because, although the 'S' was a good old chariot, we really wanted to get back to something that would stir the emotions like the E-type. We wanted a style with a 'wow' factor, a car for the younger chap rather than the older man's carriage that the 'S' had become – this became Clay 4. We also looked at a 'progressive' 'S'-derived car but using more fashionable cues – this became Clay 3. Then we looked at a 'radical' approach, something avant-garde and flamboyant to test the water and move away from the traditions of Jaguar – this would become Clay 2."

"I'm not necessarily a traditionalist," states Styling Director Geoff Lawson, "but I do have a strong belief in the legacy and the heritage that Sir William left us. I think you ignore that at your peril, but that isn't to say one or two of your sketch designs shouldn't challenge that. We're very close to our customers and we've a very strong pedigree in tradition, and if you put those two facts together it does tend to focus the way you think. But that shouldn't prevent you from looking at the other ends of the spectrum.

"If you have been with the company for some time, you appreciate the elements that make a Jaguar a Jaguar. You don't need to study them to understand them. It happens by osmosis, by culture. There are all sorts of elements in this, not just the style."

"Having decided upon four themes," continues Pollock, "we looked at sketch proposals, involving everyone in the department. We then realised that we needed further alternatives and encouraged Ford, and their European styling studio, Ghia, to help. We wrote briefs for them based on our four themes. We developed the four proposals in clay form, and they were assessed in March 1992 at a Jaguar Styling Committee review, where it was decided to abandon the 'progressive' Clay 3. More work was done on the other three, and at a further review in June Clay 1 was knocked on the head. In July the two remaining styles went through a photographic clinic in America which favoured the 'evocative' Clay 4, with E-type echoes.

"So the basic styling theme was established by July 1992, but we needed more choice. An alternative but

Clay A adopted the distinctive elliptical mouth of the D-type, E-type, XJ13 and XJ220.

essentially similar design, known as Clay A, was created. This was an attempt to improve on Clay 4, which henceforth became known as Clay M. One criticism was that the boot was too long: although this was based on the 'S' floorpan in its entirety, the feeling was that we could improve the overall balance of the car proportionately if we cropped it. So styling licence was taken and Clay A

was shortened front and rear to give a more close-coupled look."

"The Jaguar community," reflects Geoff Lawson, "were very keen to have a car that captures the spirit of the great cars of the past. Basically simple, sculptural and evocative, but modern. A new statement, but one that's still clearly traceable through its family back to the E-type

"ranged from traditional to completely off the wall – throw the book away, don't use any Jaguar cues". This latter approach was motivated by the feeling that perhaps people were bored with Jaguar interiors. The five proposals, denoted by letters A to E, can be summarised like this: 'traditional', which was saloon-derived; 'progressive', with a spinal character; 'evolutionary', with its roots in the saloon; 'avant-garde', without wood; and 'radical', which was based on a completely new direction.

Five half-scale clay models were developed from these themes and presented at the March review. Style B, the progressive version, was chosen as being worthy of taking forward but, as with the exterior, an alternative was then created to give more choice. In June the alternative, which featured the 'Spitfire wing' dashboard, as it has become known, was selected.

On 10 October 1992 a research clinic for the exteriors was carried out in great secrecy at the NEC, near Birmingham, using carefully selected members of the public. Clays A and M were displayed together with several competitor cars, all painted silver with the badges removed and glass blacked out in order to concentrate participants' minds on the style. As the Convertible was running late, photographs were used.

"The clinic ratings were neck and neck," recalls Pollock. "Where the shorter car scored was in Convertible form. It was thought to be more modern."

Research was important to support the views of Jaguar management. Having 300 potential customers come to much the same conclusions was compelling. Six days after the NEC clinic, which Lawson describes as a "rubber-stamping process", a further top management review took place and Clay A was approved.

Bill Hayden had been Chairman of Jaguar since July 1990. A no-nonsense manufacturing man with a lifetime in the industry with Ford, he was shocked by the archaic Jaguar plants and shook the company to the core with his relentless drive for quality improvements. He retired in March 1992 and was succeeded by another Englishman who had risen through Ford. Nick Scheele

at the front, the XJ220 at the back – muscles, undecorated sculptural forms with no add-ons, nothing gratuitous. A nice blend of traditional, evocative elements done in a fresh way."

Interior designs were created in parallel with the exterior styling work. For this aspect no fewer than five strategies were defined which, in Pollock's words,

Now covered in Dinoc material to give the effect of a painted body (far left), Clay A starts to sparkle. It would change in many detail ways but the basic shape was established.

Similar side view of Clay 4, now renamed Clay M, shows what a large car it looks, yet the difference is only a few inches at the rear. With its small, styled bumpers and less rounded appearance, it is more formal than Clay A. In a sense Clay A cheated, for styling licence was taken to crop the floor: Clay M honoured the original brief to retain the XJS floorpan unchanged, which explains its lengthy overhang at the rear.

In parallel with X100's exterior design, interior sketches led to five concepts modelled in half-scale. Style A was saloon-derived, a traditional design. It was to prove unacceptable.

The term 'evolutionary' was applied to Style C, which had a traditional binnacle and generous areas of wood on the doors. It was not favoured at the March review.

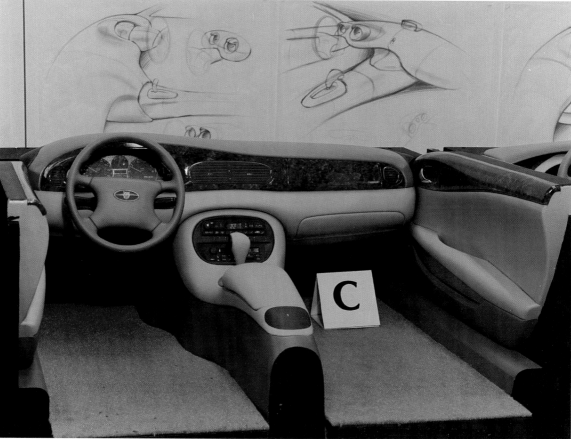

had been Managing Director of Ford Mexico until he moved to Coventry.

"Nick arrived here at a very important stage in the X100 programme," comments Mike Dale. "He possesses a great deal of corporate courage, and took up arms on behalf of his new Jaguar colleagues to make sure that we built what we believed in. I think it's greatly to Nick's credit that he argued so clearly and forthrightly. It's also greatly to their credit that Ford management listened."

Although Clay A had been selected, approval of the X100 programme was by no means a foregone conclusion. Jaguar management could not feel confident that the car would necessarily reach fruition, unless it made business sense.

Around this time Jim Padilla, a vastly experienced and charismatic senior Ford engineering man, was seconded to Jaguar. He soon installed a radical new management system for Jaguar Engineering based on a matrix structure and the formation of Heavyweight Programme Management.

"The X100 was a vehicle concept that everybody was keenly interested in," says Padilla, "including all the senior people at Ford Motor Company. There was a great deal of controversy regarding the styling and a great deal of apprehension. From the standpoint of the Jaguar team and Jaguar loyalists, that apprehension was based on a concern that Ford might unduly influence the Jaguar ethos and the Jaguarness of the product.

"What worked best was that the Jaguar team pulled together what was clearly the best style, working in a very competitive situation. The run-off was between two alternative models, both of which were Whitley-based – and the ultimate design came at the last minute. We all loved it and the market research was just outstanding. That was a very pleasing result because it removed all of the apprehension – it was truly a Jaguar-based style.

"We were left rather short on lead time to execute the programme, but the Jaguar team stepped up to that and we worked very well with some of the new processes that Ford had available to release the surfaces and get it out on time.

"This is really the second phase of what we have been trying to do in our total product orientation. Nick Scheele and I arrived at Jaguar at much the same time and we shared objectives. One of our major objectives was to avoid making Jaguar a clone of Ford. Our goal was to make Jaguar a better Jaguar. So we didn't go out and recruit loads of Ford people – we have only a handful. That was very deliberate because the heart and soul of Jaguar resides in the people, and we have exceptionally good people.

"So we decided that our focus had to be on product, product, product and quality. Phase One was the X300 and we put together the strongest product programme for a very reasonable investment. Phase Two of the programme was to put together a rejuvenation of the sports

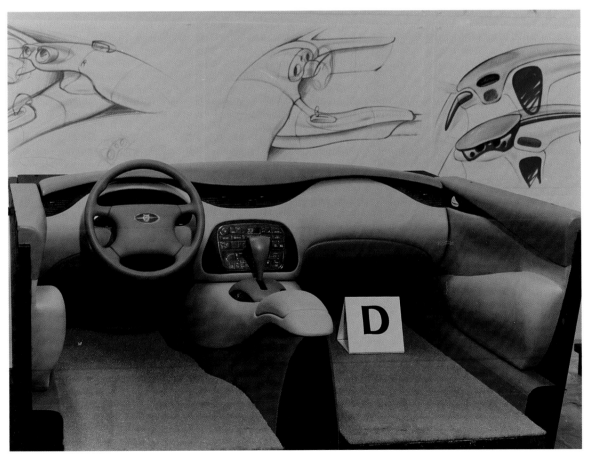

Style D eschewed wood completely and was avant-garde. Not surprisingly, it met an instant death, which must have been the kindest thing that could have happened to it.

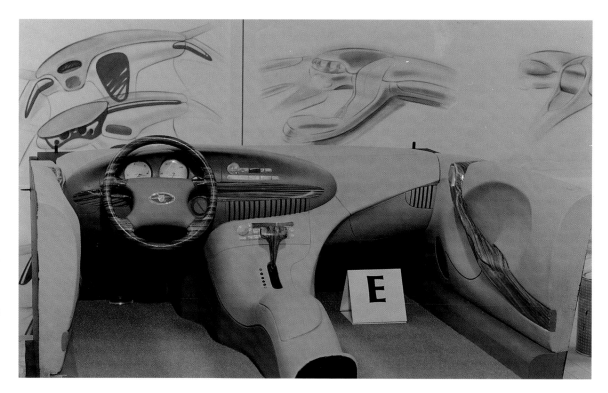

The only thing that can be said of Style E, the appropriately-named 'radical' proposal, is that it was even more extreme that D! One cannot help but think of the grand old Duke of Wellington who once said, paraphrasing slightly, "I don't know what effect this will have on the enemy, but by God it terrifies me!"

Style B could be termed 'progressive' and had a spinal theme with an enormous centre console that wrapped over the dash. This was chosen at the March review – the other four were consigned to oblivion – but bears no resemblance to the production version.

car – the X100 and an all-new V8 engine. Phase Three will be even more new products.

"We had just brought project management into Jaguar and deployed that on our X300 programme. We looked around for a strong leader within Jaguar to manage the X100 project. Bob Dover was the choice, and a very good one given his strong product and manufacturing background."

Bob Dover's background includes lengthy spells with Pressed Steel and Massey Ferguson, for whom he worked in the US, South Africa, Poland and France. He then joined Land Rover as Manufacturing Director and was the Project Director for the successful Discovery. He joined Jaguar in 1986 as Manufacturing Director.

There is an infectious enthusiasm and drive within Jaguar now, and no-one radiates this more than David Hudson. A down to earth man, his responsibilities are the three manufacturing plants in Coventry and Birmingham, for car assembly at Browns Lane, engines at Radford and bodies at Castle Bromwich.

"For me," says Hudson, "the whole vehicle for change has been Jim Padilla. The two biggest 'chimneys' have traditionally been Manufacturing and Product Engineering. Jim Padilla broke the chimneys down, supported by Clive Ennos. We are actually now worrying about the product most of the time, instead of worrying about scoring points off each other, which maybe was the traditional approach.

"When the X100 Project Team was formed under Bob Dover, I had representation. Tim Brear became my man on that team. He still reported to me but he was on Bob's team 100% of the time. So he would return to home base every Monday morning, for my weekly management briefing. He would tell us what they would be looking at that week – it might, for example, be water leaks or squeaks and rattles – and state that he wanted some help and expertise because they would be deciding what they needed in the car. We would decide who was the best person to go and represent the plant's needs. We were in there very early on, which could make all the difference."

"In the old days," recalls Ennos, "a car would be styled and then handed across for Engineering to design the bits you can't see. What's patently obvious to us now, but wasn't then, is that Manufacturing then come

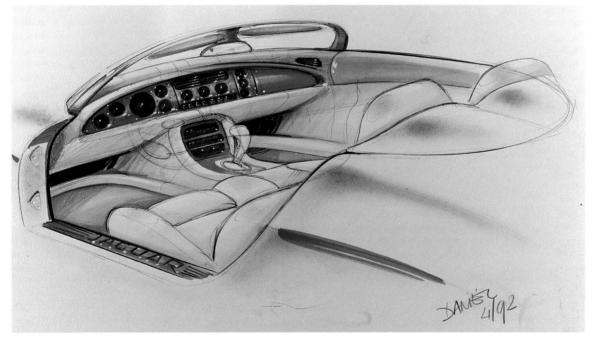

As with the exterior styles, an alternative interior was then sought to offer more choice. This wooden dash (above), very bold but evocative, seemed like good progress. In a later sketch (left) the same basic theme had been toned down, and was very close to the chosen style. The wooden dash would become known internally as the 'Spitfire wing'.

back and say there's something they can't make. So the style has to be changed and becomes compromised in localised areas.

"So virtually the minute the stylist starts to shape clay, there has to be somebody with him saying, 'Yes, that's feasible. You can do these lamp treatments. It's difficult for us to form the metal round there, but we think we can do that.'

"That's fundamental to you arriving at the Jaguar style. Jaguar style is unique, and very demanding. Most large manufacturers would take one look at the X100

bonnet and say 'we're not going to make that!' It really is difficult. But if you get the manufacturing guys sold on the project early, they love the look of it as well. Then they and the engineers are all motivated to find a way, with some clever tooling, to get it made. If you just present them with it, they'll say, 'If you'd talked to us, we'd have told you it can't be done'. On X100, using the Project Team, we really had them involved right up front.

"When we first looked at X100, we weren't sure whether we could make it feasible, particularly around the lamps, and lots of meetings went on. But the whole ethos of the meetings was so positive: how can we find a way of making this because it looks so damned good?"

"Coming up with a concept is quite difficult," states styling supremo Lawson. "But getting it approved – that's hard. And then making it 100% for world legislation – that's really tough. That's when all your cost, servicing, marketing, manufacturing and paintshop issues come to the surface, and usually the input during that time will only degrade the integrity of the original design. To hang on to the integrity of that original design so that it looks more or less the way you wanted it is just plain hard work. There's not much inspiration at that stage – it's perspiration.

"Fergus Pollock's role as our manager is to stand and fight his corner, but he has to know when to back off. There's no point in a car looking great if we can't make it, and no point in making it if it looks awful."

Once the exterior shape had been finalised, the clay was digitised – a process that maps the surface in three dimensions – by the CAD (Computer Aided Design) experts. This team, led by Steve Smith, employed the latest mathematical surface modelling technology called ICEM SURF. This software enabled the engineers to develop further the engineering and manufacturing feasibility of the approved shape. Although many subtle dimensional changes were made, the original design intent was retained. Due to the pressure on time, Smith and five colleagues would develop their designs by the end of given days, so that a model could be milled overnight for review the next morning.

Another key member of the Project Team was Keith Adams, whose province is Timing. "We were trying to learn from Ford about how to deliver a better product more quickly. Ford was operating its Concept To

The two remaining contenders, Clays A and M, were taken to a secret styling clinic at the NEC, Birmingham, in October 1992 to be judged against each other and the competition. To create a level playing field, the cars were all painted silver, glass was blacked out and badges were removed. By now Clay M (above) had been reworked to resemble Clay A (below) at the front. The XJS, which had to last another four years, was included for comparison.

Customer process, the thread of which is to have a number of very disciplined Gateways and measurement points to judge progress, and to align the process with very specific prototype phases."

Prototype work generally split into four stages: Simulators, Mechanical Prototypes, Evaluation Prototypes and Verification Prototypes. The Simulators, or workhorses, basically undertook initial single-system simulation, and XJSs containing X100 systems were used mainly because they were convenient. A full listing of these Simulators, which were built in late 1992 and early 1993, can be found on pages 126-127, together with details of all later prototypes.

"One of our roles in Prototype," says Ian Minards, the team member who supervised the construction of all prototypes, "is to build package aids, like ergonomic bucks – physical representations of the interior of the car to assess ergonomics. These help the CAD operators to make physical representations of their designs, using the Mecof machine and model-makers. The Mecof is a five-axis CNC machine that takes CAD data and cuts very accurate models.

"The engineering buck was laid down in October 1992 and it's still there to this day, having gone through a number of iterations. It's set on a Stiefelmeyer table – a big flat table with measuring arms. We built the buck up part by part, panel by panel. We made panels from vacuum formings and from steel using hammer forms to build up this representation long before we made the first prototype that looked like the real thing.

"In late 1992 MGA, the automotive design consultants, came in and took a full-size mould off the Coupé clay so that we could then make glass-fibre exteriors. That was a tough decision because there was a risk of

In spite of Clay M appearing, with hindsight, to be excessively long, the clinic scores achieved by both styles were remarkably similar in coupé form. A convertible had yet to be modelled at this stage, so images of the two choices were shown.

The heaviness of the tail on Clay A was reduced not only by shortening it, but also by the use of a dark grey bumper moulding. Another feature that would change is the door handle style used on both proposals.

When Clay A and M styles were presented 'halved' on a single full-size convertible model, Clay A received higher scores. The choices are like a slimming advert showing 'before' and 'after'! From the front, Clay A is lower and more sporty, but at this stage both had a badge on the splitter bar, à la E-type. Six days after the NEC clinic, Clay A was chosen.

damaging the clay. Later, when the Convertible clay was finished, we took a 'splash' off the back end of that so we could graft the two together.

"We achieved a number of things from this exercise. Firstly, we got an aerodynamic simulator (SIM 15), which was just a rolling platform with a GRP Coupé body structure. The front of the cooling Simulator came out of this mould as well. And we built two show cars, although again they were not runners."

At the end of October 1992 a small group, including Bob Dover, spent some time at Ford's Dearborn operation. There they were to learn about Rapid Product Development and benchmark what was regarded as the best ever new car programme in North America – the SN95 New Mustang. This had parallels with the X100 project: there were coupé and convertible versions with an element of carry-over from the previous model, together with a tight budget and a challenging time scale. Not everyone within Ford was overjoyed by the acquisition of Jaguar, which, with its mounting losses, could be seen to be restricting investment elsewhere, but the Mustang team could not have more helpful.

"Will Boddie and John Coletti," says Dover, "shared all of their thinking with us, let us sit in at their meetings, allowed us to drive their CP2 prototype, and stayed with

us for breakfast, lunch and dinner. We would continue to talk into the night. On the 'plane back I started to analyse some of the Mustang lessons that would change the shape of our X100 programme."

In November Dover started a series of Early Sourcing meetings to select all the component or system suppliers and give them a Design Brief, which would define their terms of reference for quality, function, timing and cost. The first major change was made to the programme when it was decided not to use the XJS rear suspension, which dated back to the E-type but which the floorpan was designed to accept. Instead it was decided to fit the X300 suspension, which would entail tooling changes to the rear structure.

As for body tooling, Dover was keen to use a single supplier for tooling feasibility, tool specification, tool manufacture and panel manufacture. Additionally his plan was to obtain the assembly tooling as part of the same package in order to maximise 'synergy'. He also wanted to use two of the techniques – Master Locations and No Adjust Car Build – he had seen so effectively employed on the Mustang project, so supplier experience of this technique was also an important factor.

Dover had hoped to place this work with one of the Ford toolrooms but, with all the new Ford programmes

The 'Spitfire wing' proposal was modelled and received Board approval, together with Clay A, in October 1992.

With the basic interior theme established, a further variation – with bolder white-faced dials – was examined, but Jaguar decided to retain its more traditional approach.

going through, none had sufficient capacity. Consequently on 16 December he recommended to the Jaguar Board that the contract be placed with Ogihara of Japan, the largest independent toolmaker in the world and a company that had met exceptional deadlines on the Mustang programme. The deal was agreed, in principle, within five days.

So much work had gone on through 1992, but as the year closed the X100 programme still had to be approved by the Jaguar and Ford Boards. It was by no means certain that the new sports car would actually see light of day. On 19 December, however, Bob Dover and his colleagues met for the first time an individual who was to be key to the programme.

"Wayne Booker, a very senior Ford man, was to take responsibility for Jaguar," says Dover, "and was to be a major driving force in Jaguar's return to profitability. On his first viewing of the clay models, he was supportive. His comment, 'How can we get this approved?', kept us going through the dark days ahead."

In late 1992 a mould was taken off the master clay by design consultants MGA. This enabled a glass-fibre styling model to be built early in 1993 for show purposes.

X100 EDGES TOWARDS PROGRAMME APPROVAL – 1993

Jaguar entered 1993 with the styling for the X100 Coupé and Convertible now approved, but the programme itself was by no means certain to come to fruition.

The second full calendar year of the X100 programme, 1993, was to prove a tense and critical one in the story of Jaguar's embryonic new sports car, to say nothing of the very company itself.

At the beginning of 1993 good progress was being made on the X100 design and the first examples of the 24 Simulators had been completed. Suppliers were being encouraged to develop their components or systems to support the project, which was planned for launch in 1996. Meanwhile, some development funds were found and a task early in the new year was to organise a local supplier for the prototype body panels. By mid-January six engineers from Ogihara were working at Whitley on production tooling feasibility even though there were no funds to pay for this; the goodwill extended by Ogihara, as a result of its previous dealings with Nick Scheele, would prove invaluable.

During February the first results of wind tunnel testing with the glass-fibre mock-up indicated that work was required to the bumpers to reduce rear-end lift. On 9 February the clays were shown to the US Dealer Council, who wanted a leather hood cover, wire wheels and a chrome screen surround, but nevertheless gave the team a standing ovation. During the third week of the month, Bob Dover had his first experience of the new AJ26 V8 engine with the five-speed transmission which had been fitted into an XJ40 shell. He found the engine noisy and the gearbox incorrectly calibrated, but the torque curve was excellent. On 24 February Chris Leadbeater was appointed Convertible Manager.

"When we started," recalls Leadbeater, "we were going to use a steel hood frame, but Karmann, our chosen supplier, believe aluminium frames are the way of the future. We had some discussions and it was thought to provide a better long-term solution overall. Clearly there's a significant weight saving, personally I think die-cast aluminium looks better than fabricated steel, and with casting it's easier to achieve dimensional control over the elements of the hood frame."

Also during February Dover showed the clays to several Trades Union leaders. At a Product Committee meeting late in the month he failed to secure approval for more budget. MGA were then contracted to make two full-size rolling models on XJS chassis for forthcoming US Ford meetings. In the coming months these glass-fibre models would cross the Atlantic at least five times.

Meanwhile work continued on the car's design even though it was by no means certain whether it would ever see light of day. Mark White, together with John Williams, was responsible for the body structure design, or body-in-white as it is known in the business.

"Stiffness equals refinement," states White. "The stiffer the body, the more refined the car. There's a stiffness versus weight compromise, but you can optimise stiffness without affecting weight. In fact, you can increase the stiffness and decrease the weight at the same time."

"We came up with a concept design for the car that was obviously driven by the style and the package. We then analysed that, and this is the first project where we've used computer analysis as a driving tool as opposed to a retrospective verification tool. So I worked very closely with Brian Nightingale, who is in charge of the analysis section, and we bounced ideas off each other. My guys would do an idea for a joint or a structure. They would ask, 'What if you did this? What if you do that?'. We'd then go away and make a change, and then give them the final version to analyse. They would come back and suggest further improvements, and my guys would then take that stress information and modify the overall design.

"The target, a minimum of 10% better than the XJS Coupé and Convertible, was quite an ambitious one bearing in mind that the XJS Convertible was the best in class for torsional stiffness. We also set ourselves a good weight reduction target. So we had a double-edged sword. We wanted to increase the stiffness by 10% but we also wanted to take weight out of the car. On the X100 Convertible that was quite tricky because the XJS Convertible is quite a heavy car – it was originally

The mould formed from the styling clay in late 1992 enabled several glass-fibre shells to be made for different uses. One shell was mounted on a rolling platform and this first Simulator (SIM 15) was used in the wind tunnel for early aerodynamic work.

Early development versions of the AJ26 V8 engine were fitted into XJ40 saloons. This iteration, known as AO, saw running engines in their earliest form. The many differences include cast aluminium inlet manifolds, cast cam covers and a side-mounted throttle.

The Convertible soft-top was subjected to wind tunnel testing and, as seen in these two shots, high-speed running made the top bulge. More work was done to eradicate this tendency.

designed as a coupé and later chopped down to turn it into a convertible.

"To convert the XJS, we had had to put in double floors, sill tubes and reinforcements in areas like the dash, wheelarches and petrol tank floor. The double floors restrict foot room, so the first thing we did on the X100 concept design was remove the stiffeners to create more space. We then analysed with and without the stiffeners, and looked at the key sensitive areas. We assessed what we could do with either panel up-gauge or adding a few highly stressed reinforcements, but using much smaller parts. When we did that, we actually bettered the XJS underframe.

"That allowed us to take out the double floors and most of the convertible reinforcements. Because the XJS was altered to be a convertible later, its manufacture also involved miles of CO_2 welding. We were able to reduce this by over 60%, mainly because we took out many of the reinforcements. We also reduced the number of panels in both versions by over 30%, and this significantly cut down the amount of weld involved. So it was plus, plus, plus at the start of the programme."

In early March, Scheele and Dover were preparing a paper for the Ford 'Triannual' meeting. At a preview with Wayne Booker it became obvious that there were concerns about costs, investment, volumes, prices and market share. Bob Dover, Martin Broomer and Finance Manager Tony Duckhouse worked through the night on

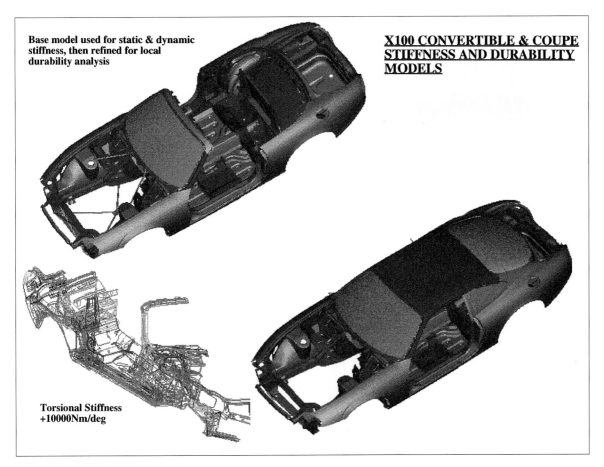

Base model used for static & dynamic stiffness, then refined for local durability analysis

X100 CONVERTIBLE & COUPE STIFFNESS AND DURABILITY MODELS

Torsional Stiffness
+10000Nm/deg

One of the principal aims of the team designing the body structure was to increase stiffness, which would benefit refinement. The XJS Convertible suffered from the fact that the car was designed as a coupé and later metamorphosed into a convertible. Computer analysis allowed the engineers to optimise the new design.

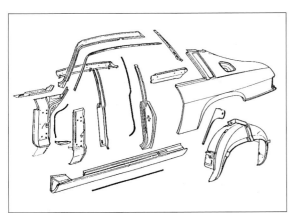

Another fundamental target, prior to the X300, was to cut down the number of body panels involved in construction, thereby reducing complexity and manufacturing time. Jaguars had traditionally been constructed from many small panels, which kept down the initial cost of tooling but increased manufacturing time and hampered quality.

revisions and alternatives. The stark choices, in Dover's words, were these: "Do nothing, do a legal upgrade only on the XJS, fit the AJ26 engine into the XJS only, fit the engine and freshen the XJS yet again, and, finally, drop the Coupé altogether and just build the Convertible with a hard-top option to reduce investment". On the morning of 16 March, the night's work was reviewed with Jim Padilla, who suggested some further refinements. In the middle of this the full-size models had arrived from MGA and, as one was rather unfinished, Styling had worked until 3am as well...

"The Triannual Reviews," explains Dover, "had grown from informal reviews ahead of Ford Board meetings to significant and highly choreographed business reviews.

Jaguar remained a small part of this European event. The financial climate couldn't have been worse. At the 19 February meeting with Ford in London, our Finance Director, John Edwards, had advised of a deterioration in projected Jaguar losses.

"The X100 was the first presentation. The Jaguar Board sat behind senior Ford executives Red Poling, Alan Gilmour, Alex Trotman and Jac Nasser, and supported magnificently. But the mood was tense."

Discussion centred on the relative importance to Jaguar of the XJ saloon – representing 80% of the business – and the replacement for the XJS. To enable major investment in the saloon, the possibility of terminating the X100 programme was considered.

The senior Ford management were merely doing their jobs. Their first professional priority was to run a successful company, and their first responsibility was to their shareholders. There was no anti-Jaguar attitude and no personal animosity during the meeting, and afterwards, in spite of the hard questioning, Poling, Gilmour and Trotman congratulated Dover on the presentation.

Meanwhile, valuable time on what was already a tight programme was being lost. Numerous further meetings took place as Jaguar worked to develop its strategy for keeping X100 alive. Mike Beasley came up with a number of ideas and welcome cost reductions, while Bob Dover, Martin Broomer and colleagues continued to comb through every single component to reduce cost wherever possible.

Most of the team were kept in the dark, intentionally, about the true situation to keep them motivated. Certain suppliers were still supporting the programme as an act of faith and the engineering team were pressing on. The 22 XJS and two XJ40 Simulators were being put to good use with nine used for engine testing and further examples for driveline, cooling, in-car entertainment systems, air conditioning and crash testing. The suspension was being evaluated on a special buggy.

"One of the most interesting of the Simulators was SIM 13," recalls Ian Minards. "This was the car that was pictured in the press doing high-speed testing at Nardo in Italy. It was an XJS with an AJ26 engine and an X100 glass-fibre front, which had to be fitted to make the front of the car representative for high-speed cooling tests."

Ken Heap heads the team that was responsible for suspension and braking systems. During 1992 and '93 this team had been making progress, as he explains. "We

define the kinds of geometries we want at the start and then go through a couple of iterations while we're looking at the packaging. That forces changes to the geometries, which you then have to bring back to where you want them to be. Then you get into the detail definition of things like the cross-beam and mounting systems, while all the time you're keeping track of the progress of the overall package.

"Initially we had the XJS underframe as a 'given', so the front suspension had to be substitutional within that body structure. The engine was the biggest problem because it had to go quite far forward in the engine bay, dictated by the bank angle of the V8. The sump is at the front of the engine whereas the six-cylinder and V12

Once the styling clay had been approved, it was digitised, the surface-smoothers took out all irregularities and further feasibility work was done. A further model was then milled, using a Mecof five-axis cutting machine, and painted black in order to check the highlights and ensure that the integrity of the original had been preserved. The approved clay could be termed the 'styling intent' model and the Mecof model (seen here) the 'production intent' example.

During 1993 24 Simulators were built. Most of these XJS-based cars were indistinguishable from normal production cars, but SIM 13, completed in March, was given a glass-fibre X100 front end because it was to be used for cooling tests.

The advantage of using XJS lookalike cars was that they could be tested without camouflage, but for cooling work it was necessary to run the true, unadorned shape. As a consequence SIM 13 was caught by telephoto lenses while at Nardo, Italy, and appeared in the press.

engines had the sump at the back, so that it sat behind the front suspension cross-member."

Very early on, in fact, there had been thoughts of using the X300 underframe instead, but the longitudinal members are higher on the saloon and effectively ruled out this avenue. The possibility of carrying the XJS structure over to X300 was also examined, so that the new saloon would share exactly the same suspension with X100. However, apart from the height difference of the longitudinals, those on the XJS actually splay wider to the front in plan view. Consideration was then given to a modular cross-beam with basic common elements but with different upper wishbone mountings. As a result of

the higher volume resulting from this component being common to both ranges, manufacturing the cross-beam in pressed steel would have made commercial sense.

"Very soon it became obvious that the compromises were just too great," continues Heap. "We couldn't produce a satisfactory cross-beam to serve both cars, so we had to forget it. While X300 would be done differently, X100 would go with XJS and have a dedicated front suspension cross-beam.

"We considered aluminium for this cross-beam because the lifetime volume of X100 would be relatively small and the tooling cost of aluminium is much lower than steel. The unit costs with aluminium are a little

This buggy, built by Jaguar engineers to assess and develop new suspension systems, offers two important advantages. First, it frees up an expensive prototype for work where the majority of the car must be representative. Second, its totally over-engineered structure allows suspension testing to be far more destructive.

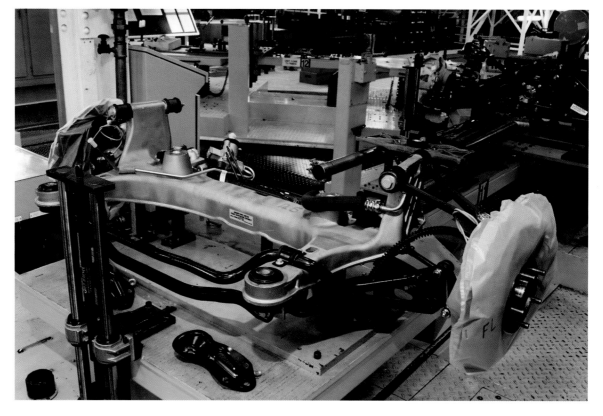

New front suspension, employing conventional top and bottom wishbones, was designed and developed for the X100. Reduced weight and ground offset were two of the targets the engineers set for themselves and achieved.

higher, but over the lifetime volume it breaks even. We did actually start with a pressed steel beam and had prototypes made, but we had a bad pressing and welding condition in one corner of the beam, and we couldn't make the joint live with fatigue. That factor, combined with the aluminium weight advantage, made it a 'no brains decision'.

"We could fix the fatigue issue with aluminium. With a casting you can obviously put the metal where it is most needed, and there are none of the material discontinuities that arise with welding. So the structure becomes much more homogeneous, and in many ways more efficient. The steel beam weighed 21-22kg, but the aluminium one is under 15kg. It's a lovely piece of kit.

"Once we had the beam sorted, the suspension linkages were developed. We have continued with traditional Jaguar high-tensile forged steel, but we did a great deal of FE [Finite Element] and load analysis on the design of these parts to absolutely minimise their cross-sections, and therefore their weight.

"Considerable work went into packaging the vertical link because we wanted to reduce the ground offset to lessen the car's sensitivity to longitudinal inputs, such as braking. The XJS, grand old girl that she is, has a very high ground offset. That's historical because it dates back to the sixties when the original XJ6 was engineered. In those days ground offset wasn't considered to be significant, whereas today we know it is. That was one of the things we very much wanted to improve upon."

In May Joe Greenwell of the PR department was promoted to head up Overseas Sales and Martin Broomer replaced him as Manager, Product Affairs. Phil Hodgkinson in turn took over from Broomer in the Sports Car Programme Office.

Still the X100 programme remained uncertain, awaiting approval from the Ford Board, and by late May another 'economy' proposal had been prepared for a

"On 25 May, at 7.15 in the morning, I met Jim Padilla making coffee," recollects Dover. "There had been an overnight message from Ford that Wayne Booker and Alex Trotman would be supporting our cycle plan, and the X100 would be supported as a Sales & Marketing dealer protection plan. We had, of course, included dire warnings as to what would happen to our dealers if Jaguar became a saloon-only franchise."

In spite of the uncertainty about X100, work was still progressing on the new sports car. The convertible model stack was 'signed off', or approved, and after two days with suppliers ITT and Valeo, the bumpers and headlamp unit dimensions were finalised. Problems at this stage included a lack of cooling, difficulty packaging the anti-roll bar and late delivery of parts for the Mechanical Prototypes, the next prototype stage for which build was scheduled to take place in late 1993 and early 1994.

On 9 June several members of the Ford Board met Prime Minister John Major and Michael Heseltine, at that time the Government Minister responsible for Trade, to discuss the same kind of assistance that the British Government had provided to Nissan for its plant in Washington, Tyne & Wear. The proposed Board minutes a few days later made it very clear that Ford approval for the new V8 engine and the X100 were subject to the receipt of commitments for appropriate financial assistance from the British Government.

"So the situation couldn't have been clearer," says Dover. "No grant would mean no V8 engine and no X100. We started to pull together a grant application. Meanwhile we were still trying to take cost out of the project. We tried to sort out the minimum long-lead orders and agreed a minor styling revision for to the front bumper."

After Dover visited the long-lead suppliers – ITT, Karmann and Valeo – to keep the timing, cost and design activities going, the two glass-fibre models of X100 in Coupé and Convertible guises were used for further clinics demanded by Ford. Run by Ford and ultra-professional, these took place on the ground floor of a multi-storey car park in Los Angeles. Following the number-crunching of all the scores, Ford found to its amazement that the figures for X100 were the highest it had seen!

"One of the key findings from our research," recalls Dover with amusement, "was the requirement to have a height-rise mechanism on the seat. I will never forget an incident that occurred when Fergus Pollock and I were in that multi-storey car park in deepest Los Angeles – it really was the most grim location you could imagine. I

Integral to the new front suspension is this cast aluminium front beam, which was wholly designed on computer and, unlike the fabricated steel prototype beams that preceded it, passed every structural test thrown at it.

model codenamed NPX. This was merely a reskinned XJS with a potential for 2000 sales per annum at an investment of around £70 million. At much the same time Scheele and Padilla had given their colleagues in the US a superb presentation on X100 and fielded 90 minutes of questions. The project was put 'on hold', which at least was better than being cancelled.

*While the
suspension
engineers were
stressing and
analysing their
components,
body-in-white
colleagues were
carrying out
similar computer
studies on the
body structure
to determine
the effect of
suspension loads
on the mounting
points.*

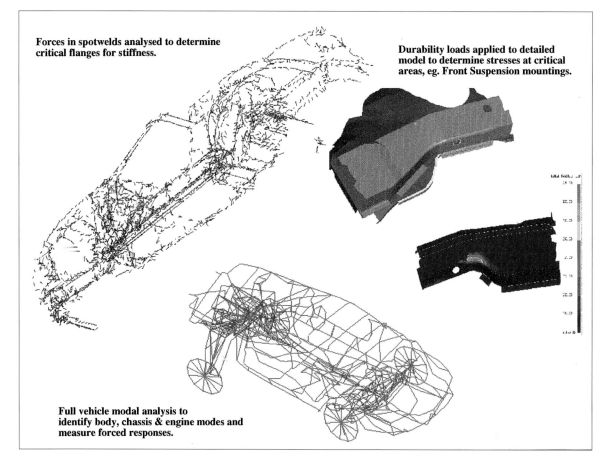

Forces in spotwelds analysed to determine critical flanges for stiffness.

Durability loads applied to detailed model to determine stresses at critical areas, eg. Front Suspension mountings.

Full vehicle modal analysis to identify body, chassis & engine modes and measure forced responses.

remember this lovely, small American lady, who I guess was exactly the right age and background for our typical customer, saying, 'I love this car but I can't see over the steering wheel'. After that we couldn't avoid putting in a seat height-riser – that decision cost about £2.5 million!"

On 7 July Michael Heseltine's junior minister wrote to say that there would be no grant for X100 as it would be built anyway. There was a suggestion from elsewhere that the Welsh Office might help as the decision had been taken to manufacture the engine at Ford's Bridgend plant in South Wales, but there was little optimism. Meanwhile all funds for the X100 project were frozen. At the British Grand Prix that weekend rumours circulated that the 'XJS replacement' had been cancelled.

Following the negative reaction to requests for British Government aid, Ford decided that plants in other countries would be considered for the manufacture of X100, and maybe other Jaguars too. In the past Ford had received very positive support from the Portuguese Government and so its plant at Azambuja was considered. Jaguar undertook an extensive study of all the factors and found that, without grants, manufacture in Portugal would be more expensive than in the UK.

Meanwhile Nick Scheele was becoming very concerned that unless the V8 engine was approved and an order placed imminently with the supplier of the special Nikasil plating process (see the next chapter), there would be a six-month delay. For a host of other reasons

too, the Project Team began looking at delaying X100 by that period...

Plants in the US (at Wixom) and Mexico were concurrently being considered alongside Azambuja. Wherever X100 was to be built, if it was to be built at all, any delay in waiting for grant approval would cost the company dearly in lost sales if it delayed the programme. Jaguar appeared to be in a no-win situation.

"That was a bad period altogether," recalls Scheele, "and 1993 was a terribly difficult year for Jaguar. We were still more than a year away from launching X300. People were asking why we needed a unique Jaguar engine and we had to demonstrate that. We also continued to lose money. We had some very difficult sessions through this period.

"My wife and I have a cottage on one of the great lakes near Detroit and we'd planned to take a two-week summer holiday there. But the X100 programme still had to be fought for in Detroit, so Bob Dover ended up staying with us for most of the holiday. Of the 14 days I was supposed to have at the cottage, I think I spent about nine in Detroit. Jim Padilla was also supposedly on holiday in Dearborn and gave up his vacation too.

"There was a sense of horror among my colleagues at the thought of a Jaguar being built in Portugal. 'You can't possibly be serious?' We sent Mike Beasley off to Portugal to look at the plant, and he told the Board on his return that Azambuja would be a super plant to build

The execution of the glass-fibre styling models was to a very high standard. The windows of the Coupé were blacked out, but the Convertible had a fully detailed interior – one director even asked to look at the engine!

X100 in. He was deadly serious and you could see everybody's face drop like a stone."

Back in the UK, Dover had 14 days of non-stop meetings and then, together with Purchasing Director Paul Stokes, left for Japan. There they were to visit Nippondenso (who were supplying the engine management system and the air conditioning unit), Nishikawa (a manufacturer of seals new to Jaguar) and Ogihara (whose version of the styling model needed approval, which unfortunately could not be given because it had not been finished off correctly).

"One of the key things about a convertible is the sealing system," states Dover. "The seals have to be very durable and also slightly more tolerant than those fitted to a closed car because there is more body movement and a requirement for more tolerance for glass setting.

The two glass-fibre styling models thoroughly earned their keep, crossing to the USA and back at least five times to appear at clinics, meetings and reviews. Note the dark grey rear bumper.

The styling models were also used in the wind tunnel and it can be seen that a small front chin spoiler was tried. Generally the shape performed well and only small tweaks were needed, allowing the shape to remain pleasingly clean.

We benchmarked 10 convertibles and found that five of them used a sponge seal technology system supplied by Nishikawa. We had never heard of them but we decided on the evidence that this was the company to use.

"When we visited Nishikawa I took some slides of SS100s and XK120s so that they could understand a bit about our ethos. Their offices were really tacky and they clearly hadn't spent a penny on them for years. We showed them sketches of the car and they merely nodded. Paul Stokes and I were getting more and more nervous: there we were in downtown Hiroshima in the rain thinking that this wasn't such a good idea after all. It actually got worse. They then popped us in a minibus – it was clearly hired because the tyres were bald and the engineer who was driving didn't know where the controls were! – and we hared off through the rain to one of their factories. And then all the doubts disappeared.

"It was just magical. It was clear that they'd spent all their money on their processing operation. The factory was immaculately clean. The people were well trained. Each person had his training record up on the wall with his biorhythm chart so he knew when to be careful. They were making some of the most complex seals we'd ever seen. As soon as we entered the factory, we knew that we'd made the right decision – it shows how you can get the wrong impression just by looking at offices. My colleagues in Finance later gave me quite a bit of hassle because the seals are fairly expensive, but customers won't tolerate water leaks or wind noise."

Paul Stokes elaborates on the reasons for going to Japan. "Bill Hayden drove the company to keep looking

at quality. Mike Beasley will tell you that he was pursued relentlessly on the quality issue, and there was the same pressure on me to find quality suppliers. Indeed Bill Hayden had definite views on X100. Nippondenso are the best in the world. They were a benchmark company at the time on engine management systems. That, he decided, was the company we should work with."

Jaguar air conditioning systems have not always been the best, to put it kindly. It was decided to find out who supplied Lexus and ask that manufacturer what it was developing for the future. Again it was Nippondenso.

Not quite all was doom and gloom on the financial side during this period, as Ford continued to support Jaguar's capital programmes. Jim Padilla explains: "We knew we had to invest in the manufacturing facilities. We had extensive discussions on what was really core business for Jaguar. What are those things that only Jaguar can do to make a car a Jaguar? What's critical for the customer? The style, the refined power, the ride and handling balance – all these are distinctive features.

"From this we knew that only we could make the bodies, only we could paint the cars. We knew that we had to invest fundamentally in the assembly facility. So we put in a complete new facility at Browns Lane. The cost? Just 15 million bucks – bargain. The team knocked down the whole of the old assembly line that had been in there since the early fifties, that Sir William bought secondhand, and that was pre-World War II vintage! It was impossible to build quality on that.

"I talked to one of the people on the line after we put in the new facility and asked him what the biggest

For the first time in 30 years a new production line was installed, in late 1993, and this investment played a major part in improving manufacturing quality and working conditions.

difference was. He says, 'Oh, my shins!' I ask, 'Why your shins?' He says, 'You remember the old tracks. Above ground. You couldn't get the stock in so you had to carry it over two above-ground tracks. You banged your shins every third time you crossed them.' Big difference."

During September 1993, MP19, the first of the 53 Mechanical Prototypes, was completed. Although most of these cars were lookalike XJSs, MP19 was not. It was originally conceived as an air conditioning simulator, which meant it needed an X100 glasshouse. Ian Minards, who was in charge of Prototype Build, went to the body plant at Castle Bromwich one Saturday and had a bespoke XJS underframe built by deleting standard panels and supplying substitutes.

"We brought that underframe back to Whitley," explains Minards, "and fitted modified XJS front suspension, XJS rear suspension and an AJ26 engine. This gave us a rolling platform which then needed to be clad in a representative X100 body structure. We sent the rolling platform to MGA and they took another full-size 'splash' off the mould and stitched the glass-fibre body to the underframe to make a running car. What we ended up with was a car that looked like an X100 painted in a bright red colour.

"Ian and I were entrusted to make a video of this car," states Russ Varney of the Vehicle Office. "We had someone in-house to shoot the video and for security reasons I wasn't keen on telling anyone where we were going. In fact Ian and I went off on Friday afternoon, scouted round a few locations, and finally decided on a place called Flecknoe, about 20 miles away. There was a

nice little stretch of road and a few escape routes if we did get cornered."

"We went out at 5.00 one Saturday morning," continues Minards, "having put the car in a Ford Cargo truck. There were myself and Russ Varney, some fitters, my engineer who'd built the car, and Steve Davis who shot the video. It was a bit like cops and robbers as we all had radios. You can imagine that a spy photo of the car that early on would have been disastrous. We filmed for about two hours, came back, edited it – and we were pretty stunned by what it looked like.

"The next day we went to MIRA to do high-speed running and a few shots round cones. At one point we managed to lose a water hose off the engine and a great cloud of steam erupted as the car came down the main straight! We had a big white sheet to cover the car with a hole cut out for the windscreen. As we towed it back to the workshop, it looked like a ghost as the cloth was shimmering! So MP19 was a lot of fun..."

The video, which is impressively professional, was completed by Bob Dover talking to camera in the Styling Studio with the full-size Coupé and Convertible models. That video was shortly to play a crucial role...

At the beginning of October, Dover flew once more to Japan, where he was able to approve the Coupé and Convertible models at Ogihara. On the 'plane back he read that Alex Trotman was to succeed Red Poling as Chairman of Ford on 1 November. The X100 project, however, was now very close to crisis point. If approval was not gained very shortly, an October 1996 launch would be impossible.

Two further trim schemes were created for a styling review in November 1993. There was a feeling that younger buyers, particularly in Germany, might favour a less traditional approach, so grey wood and white instruments were assessed.

A tan interior was also proposed, but many considered the colour overwhelming with a walnut veneer dash. As can be seen, this was purely a styling buck for viewing the interior concept.

In December the Convertible styling model was retrimmed in another combination of colours that blended the traditional with more adventurous tones.

This was also make or break time for Bob Dover and Paul Stokes, for they had put their careers on the line. They had allowed suppliers to carry on working as an act of faith. If that faith was to prove ill-founded, they would feel honour-bound to resign. It was an example of the total commitment of senior people within Jaguar.

On 12 October a letter arrived from Portugal with a promise of between £19 million and £25 million grant aid, and the possibility of more. Meanwhile negotiations had reopened with the Department of Trade and Industry (DTI) in Britain, but no decision would be made before the end of November. On the evening of 13 October, Wayne Booker 'phoned Scheele with the good news that long-lead funds of £10 million had been approved, but that the money must not be spent in such a way that the project would be committed to either Portugal or the UK. To say that Dover and Stokes were relieved is an understatement, although Bob reckoned he would probably have to learn Portuguese...

At their December meeting, the Ford Board were to be asked to approve the new model cycle plan, including the vitally important X300 saloon.

On 1 December, word came through that the British Government would offer a grant of £9.4 million, plus additional training support. A day later Wayne Booker wrote to say, 'Thanks, but no thanks' to the Portuguese.

On 7 December the late David Boole learned that *Car* magazine planned to use spy photos of the X100 in its next issue. It was a silver car and so was almost certainly the clay or one of the clinic models. It could have been taken at MGA, Dunton or the Los Angeles clinic, but Bob Dover's hunch was a mole at Whitley.

Two days later the Ford Board met. Nick Scheele represented Jaguar. Quality was discussed and, most fortuitously, Jaguar had just overtaken BMW in the influential JD Power report on one-year-old cars. The Project Team's home video of MP19 was shown – twice. Discussion ensued. A decision was taken.

The Board of Directors of the Ford Motor Company approved the X100 programme.

The year 1993 ended on a high for the Project Team when, on 9 December, the X100 project received Programme Approval. The majority of the team are seen here. From left: Keith Adams (Programme Timing), Pete French (Powertrain), Richard Ansell (Sales & Marketing), Russ Varney (Vehicle Engineering), Iain Sturgeon (Quality), Julian Jenkins (Programme Office), Bob Dover (Chief Programme Engineer), Martin Broomer (Manager, Sports Car Programme Office), Tim Brear (Manufacturing), Chris Leadbeater (Vehicle Engineering), Dave Williams (Purchasing), Alan Jordan (Finance), Andy Murphy (Chassis Engineering), Kev Riches (BIW & Trim Engineering), Nigel Sims (BIW Tooling), Chris Bevan (Manufacturing), Fergus Pollock (Styling) and Roy Blacklaw (Bumper Systems). Missing from this photograph are Ian Minards (Prototype Build), Tony Duckhouse (Finance), Jonathan Wankling (Programme Office), Umit Koymen (Body Construction) and Mark White (BIW).

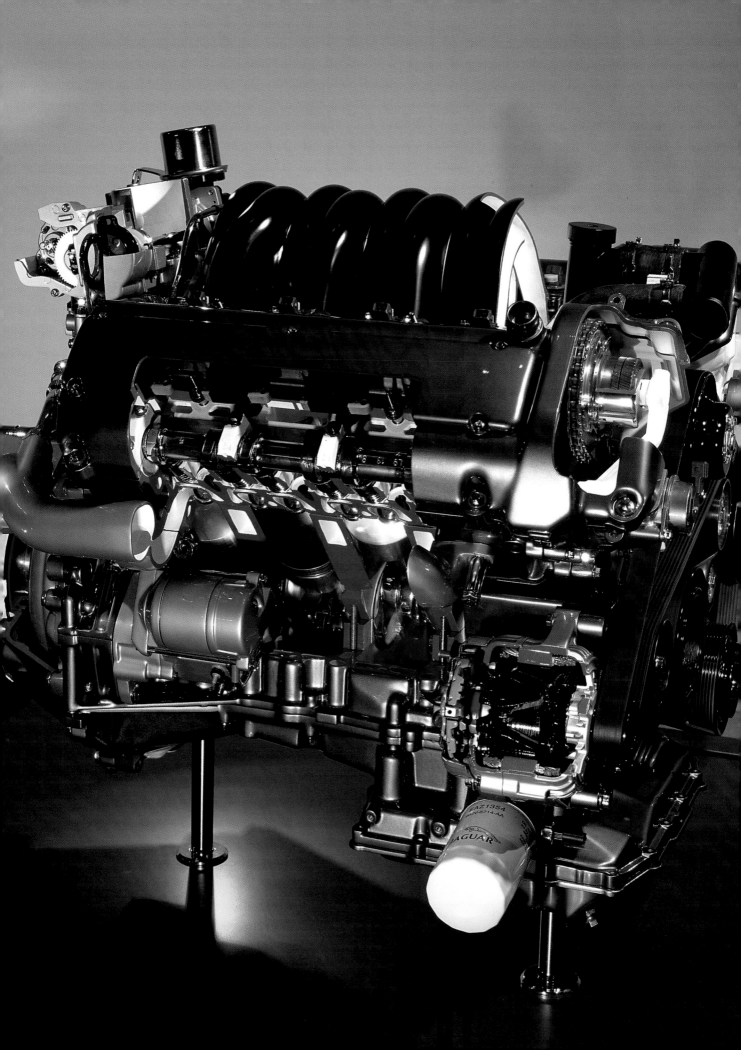

THE AJ-V8 ENGINE

"The launch of a completely new engine and transmission is an extremely rare occasion for Jaguar." The words are those of Trevor Crisp, who joined Jaguar back in 1954 and is today the powertrain Group Chief Engineer.

Back in the forties William Lyons realised that the heart of an outstanding motor car is a superb engine. He was keen to establish Jaguar at the forefront of sporting luxury cars. The XK engine, designed by such legends as Bill Heynes, Wally Hassan and Claude Baily, achieved just that and, highlighted by the Le Mans wins, Jaguar became established as an engineering force to be reckoned with. The remarkable XK engine remained in volume production until 1986.

The XK engine pioneered, for a production engine, the then innovative twin overhead camshaft design. In 1971 the XK was joined by Jaguar's brilliant V12 engine, which set new standards of smooth refinement. Being one of the world's first V12 engines to be produced in significant volume, it maintained Jaguar's image of pioneering engineering. Nobody could have predicted the fuel crises of the seventies: without the emphasis on fuel economy that resulted, it is likely that the V12 would have been produced in much greater numbers.

Innovation continued with the introduction, in 1983, of the new all-aluminium AJ6 six-cylinder engine, which saw the first use in a luxury car of four valves per cylinder technology. The AJ6 was succeeded by its offspring, the AJ16, in 1994, with the exciting supercharged version maintaining Jaguar's enterprising approach to power unit development.

"The AJ-V8 engine is only the fourth totally new concept in Jaguar's history," says Trevor Crisp. "It marks a

major step forward in both performance and technology.

"Another very significant factor is that approval for this programme, approval for spending approximately $300 million, was given by Ford after it had purchased Jaguar. This was given at a time when Jaguar was not only losing a great deal of money, but Ford was also introducing its own four-valve, all-aluminium range of modular engines. To me this clearly demonstrated not only a great faith in our engineering capability, but also Ford's determination to maintain the integrity of the Jaguar marque.

At a very early stage Dave Szczupak was appointed to manage the engine programme, and remained with it all the way through. Szczupak (pronounced Shoopack) graduated with a Masters degree from Cranfield in automotive engineering, specialising in engines, and joined Holset, the turbocharger manufacturer that is part of the Cummins Group. He moved to Jaguar in 1985 as the Power Train Manager of the Advanced Engineering group and then transferred to the mainstream design and development function as Chief Engineer.

"The V8 engine started in the late eighties," states Szczupak. "We were looking at what the next generation of Jaguar engines needed to be and how we would fulfil that requirement. There we were with a clean sheet of paper. What did our customers really want?

"Before we started our concept design work, we surveyed customers, and potential customers, right around the world. We chose our largest market, the USA, plus the UK, Germany and Japan, and asked questions about their current desires and what they wanted in the future.

"The outcome was a strong requirement in three areas. Firstly, they wanted performance and refinement –

Certain qualities of an automobile are based on subjective assessments – we all have our views. But power units are more objective and all their qualities can be measured and compared. The AJ-V8 surpasses the competition and is destined to play a very important part in Jaguar's future.

that desire to squeeze the accelerator pedal and have the car perform with ease and quietness. Secondly, our customers continued to demand very high standards of quality, reliability and durability. Thirdly, cost of ownership – both service costs and fuel economy – was an extremely important issue.

"From these customer surveys we defined a very clear message for everyone involved in the project – to

The very first AJ26 engine to be built, numbered 1001, differed from the eventual production engine in detail rather than in any major way. Notable differences include a fabricated exhaust manifold, the inlet manifold, cast cam covers and various other sand-cast parts. The accessory drive arrangement would be revised.

deliver 'Refined Power'. We would define this as a blend of performance feel, excellent low-speed torque to give that feeling of acceleration without strain, and a quiet but very pleasing sound. This combination must give a most enjoyable driving experience.

"Apart from customer inputs, there were many other market requirements. Stringent new legislation around the world includes California's low emission vehicle programme, Gas Guzzler tax, the Stage 3 European proposals on emissions, Combined Average Fuel Economy and CO_2 requirements for Europe, and drive-by noise legislation. Safety was also a consideration, since a compact engine would give the vehicle engineers the freedom to optimise front-end crash performance.

"At the start we did a lot of concept work within a small team that I managed, beginning with about 12 people and growing to about 15, including a manufacturing guy. Eventually the programme crystallised into the V8 being the proposal that we pushed ahead with."

For internal use the new engine was given the codename AJ26, but in March 1996 it was decided to christen it AJ-V8 in time for its public bow in June.

"We knew," states Trevor Crisp, "that to achieve the very challenging vehicle performance objectives for the X100, even with the anticipated high specific power out-

put of the new engine, we would still need a capacity of approximately 4 litres.

"The decision on number of cylinders was far less obvious as we had to balance the frequently conflicting requirements of refinement, cost, economy and emissions. Our market research clearly indicated that refinement was a priority, and to achieve the programme objectives for this feature we believed that we needed a minimum of eight cylinders. A short-stroke 'six' was considered but rejected due to the anticipated hydrocarbon emission problem and increased weight of the reciprocating components.

"Ten cylinders were rejected on the grounds of inherent design imbalance, and 12 cylinders for cost and increased friction giving poorer fuel consumption. By concentrating on reducing the reciprocating weight and increasing the rigidity of the engine and transmission structure, we also considered that we could obtain refinement levels equal to, or better than, our existing V12 engine. A vee configuration, of course, gives a very compact package and greater freedom of design for the whole vehicle."

David Szczupak takes up the story again. "This all started before Ford's ownership. The take-over didn't change the design, but it did change the way we managed the programme, particularly when the prospect of building the engine at Ford's Bridgend plant came along. The small group had prepared detailed concept drawings and a detailed drawing of the first V8 prototype at the point when Ford bought Jaguar, but we hadn't made any hardware. We were still very much at the concept stage.

"With Ford having a wide range of engines and a massive powertrain group, there was a great deal of dialogue and healthy debate as to whether Jaguar should continue to design this new engine – Ford was just about to launch the modular Romeo 4.6-litre V8. Why did we need to spend several hundred million on a new power unit? Why couldn't we modify a Ford engine? Trevor Crisp and I spent a lot of time in very senior level debates, mainly with Lou Ross, Vice President in charge of Ford International Operations, and hence in charge of Jaguar when it was bought.

"Lou Ross is a very keen engine guy and had been the father figure behind the Ford Romeo V8. He's a very bright man, an astute engineer and businessman. He was trying to understand Jaguar and make sure Ford made the best of it. He found a group of engineers and planners who were certain Jaguar needed a new engine – we needed to compete with Lexus, BMW and Mercedes.

"Lexus launched a fantastic new V8 engine in 1990 that really set all-new standards in terms of refinement, and BMWs are renowned for their performance – but we knew we had to exceed their achievements. Having painted the picture of the marketplace and having understood who our true competitors were, Ford realised that we had to have a bespoke engine.

"We didn't secure Ford's agreement to it by saying,

'we can build a better engine than you can'. We did it by saying, 'these are the requirements in the marketplace, and this is what an engine has to do to meet these requirements'. The project sold itself at that point.

"The Ford of Europe manufacturing team have a very strong central staff. With all Ford of Europe new engine programmes, working groups are formed out of this central group. So every time a programme finishes, that knowledge and experience goes back into the central staff. That helps create a very up-to-date experience base for delivering new programmes. They said, 'If you can get the Ford manufacturing staff to help you deliver this programme, you will have a more robust programme', something which we couldn't deny.

"So we used the Ford and Jaguar manufacturing staffs as a joint team – it was about 50/50. There were 15 key Jaguar people from Radford together with a similar number of Ford people in this core manufacturing team.

"So the great debate then was whether the engine was going to be built at Radford or Bridgend. Radford needed a lot of refurbishment. Bridgend had an empty building of ideal size, and the superb infrastructure of a completely modern, new facility. Again the decision was obvious. With Bridgend we had experience, ability and a beautiful new factory in which we could create a purpose-built, world-class Jaguar manufacturing facility."

"Emotionally it was obviously a difficult to decision to take," recalls Manufacturing Director Mike Beasley. "But from a business perspective the decision was straightforward. We knew at Jaguar that we could not build the engine in the old Radford plant: the cost to create the 'turnaround' space and the very infrastructure of the site just meant that we'd spend an absolute fortune.

"In fact, we'd already come to the conclusion that it would be cheaper for us to create a new engine plant. We were contemplating building it at Whitley and we'd drawn up some plans. With Ford's arrival, though, the expertise and infrastructure available at Bridgend – as well as the sheer economics of this solution – made the decision obvious."

"Once that was decided," continues Szczupak, "the project team had to change in terms of involving more Ford people, including the Ford quality staff. I think this is where Ford has been of most help to Jaguar generally, and to AJ26 and X100 in particular. We have learned a great deal in being able to bring modern design, management and manufacturing methods to achieve a quality approach in delivering programmes.

"So after the early concept stuff, we reached the point where we thought half a litre per cylinder was the right size, and then spent time looking at whether it should be under-square or over-square in terms of bore and stroke. In fact we built some prototype engines with 83mm bore and 92mm stroke – a traditional long-stroke engine to obtain the effortless torque that a Jaguar should always have.

Refinement was monitored in the semi-anechoic Engine Noise Test Cell (ENTC) at Whitley, Jaguar's Engineering Centre. Absorbent glass-fibre wedges minimise sound wave reflections, allowing sources of sound to be captured by four precision microphones positioned 1 metre from the engine.

Although much work can be done on test beds, it is also essential to run engines in cars. The various levels of prototypes were run in hot and cold climate extremes to assess durability and performance under demanding conditions. This development engine is fitted in MP19.

"We analysed this configuration and concluded that crankshaft stiffness wasn't sufficiently high with a long stroke. But we wanted to make sure we were going to be competitive – indeed class-leading – on refinement, so we opted for 86mm by 86mm as the compromise that still gave us as much low-speed torque but removed the crankshaft stiffness problem."

David Szczupak, who is an extremely gifted young engineer, is keen to stress the team element behind the

AJ-V8. He dislikes press stories that concentrate on the programme manager and indicate that this one individual did everything.

"The only way you develop good products is by having very good teamwork. One thing I pride myself in is helping to motivate and steer the enthusiasm and energy of the team. We have a great team of engineers at Jaguar, particularly in Power Train. The engine is only as good as it is because of the people who have put many, many hours of excellent work into it.

"The small team we formed, from people who were already at Jaguar, was quite unusual. There were some highly experienced people in their 50s and early 60s, and some straight out of university in their early 20s. There were a few people in between, but generally we had these extremes of youth and experience, and the combination worked fantastically well. I think the young, energetic, highly qualified, very intelligent guys had a healthy respect for the senior members, who in turn were open enough to want to challenge themselves. This gave us a very open, keen and energetic dialogue within the whole group."

The experienced 'wing' of the team, a few of them with backgrounds stretching to the E-type era and the latter years of the great Le Mans racing period, knew what makes a good Jaguar engine. This "controlling conservatism", in Szczupak's words, rested largely with Hugh Reddington and Joe Cooke. Reddington, the Engine Design Manager, who has since retired, arrived in 1963 when Jaguar bought Coventry Climax Engines Ltd specifically to obtain some excellent engineers, such as Wally Hassan. A real mentor to the team, Reddington had worked on the V12 during the sixties and was the mas-

termind behind the AJ6 six-cylinder. Cooke came to Jaguar even earlier, having arrived when the company purchased Daimler in 1960, and was responsible for the top end of the AJ26 engine.

And then there were the bright young engineers who will be the future of Jaguar. Nigel Massey (who looked after the bottom end), Martin Joyce and Jon Carling (who both looked after performance on the development side) were typical of the younger element, pushing hard. Analytical work blended the traditional methods of Peter Lings with the computer-based approach of Carl White and Steve Richardson, and again youthful energy and mature wisdom meshed together to propel the project that little bit further. This is by no means an exhaustive list of the key people involved, but it serves to illustrate the wide variety of skills within the team.

"You can have excellent people but you don't necessarily get an excellent product," continues Szczupak. "It's the quality of teamwork that achieves the product excellence, through people working in harmony and attending to every little detail. Until we reached the hardware stage, we actually took our people out of the main Design Office and put them into 'The Black Hole' – an office without any windows! Nobody liked it as an office, but it was somewhere where we could all get together and work closely with each other. I was the only Chief Engineer at Jaguar without an office, but my pig-pen – Jaguar parlance for a partitioned-off corner! – meant I was with the team as well."

At the same time as the team were working out how many cylinders and what capacity would be ideal, they were also looking in isolation at the optimum piston and bore/stroke ratios. A small chart itemised the fundamen-

During engine design and up-front development, considerable work was done with single-cylinder test engines to optimise bore/stroke ratio, intake and exhaust ports, combustion chamber layout, compression ratio and part-throttle Variable Cam Phasing (VCP) strategy.

tals that had to be decided, including combustion chamber and valve gear layout, whether to have direct-acting buckets or roller followers, and what valve angles and port shapes to use. The structure of the engine was being examined simultaneously, by assessing how to make the bottom end rigid, what kind of liner technology to employ, and so on. Other considerations included the engine management system (EMS), the type of fuel injection, and manifold design. All these basic areas were worked on in parallel.

It is perhaps surprising that single-cylinder test work, which was used to refine the combustion chamber design, still has a part to play in the nineties. This technique had been employed extensively in the development of the V12 engine in the sixties, and it is interesting that computer technology has not completely overtaken this type of practical experimentation.

"We can do most of our work with computers, but not all of it," says Szczupak. "We do a great deal of computer modelling, stress analysis and flow analysis, and even solidification modelling – we can actually model a casting process these days. If we have the shape of a cylinder block, we can now model the pouring of molten aluminium into the die to check that it solidifies in one direction. If it stays molten in one area and solidifies either side, shrinkage, porosity and leakage occur.

"But the one aspect that remains very difficult to model accurately is combustion, because the flow through valves is very intermittent and turbulent – and we can't yet model detonation and ignition advance accurately. Although we do have computer models of the combustion process, we use them to develop manifolds .

"So we have a simple combustion model that we use to optimise ram pipe lengths, plenum sizes, exhaust tract lengths and camshaft timing, but the single-cylinder engine is still a very important tool for studying the heart of the chamber and the gas flow into the chamber."

From being given the go-ahead to making the first prototype engine took about 12 months – quite a short period of time in the development of a new engine. Szczupak still remembers with great fondness the exciting moment when the first engine ran for the first time. Such was the team spirit, everyone had a little wager on what the power output of the first engine would be. The total bet came to about £50 and was won by Colin Lea, one of the cylinder block designers.

"The production engine hasn't changed very much from that first prototype," continues Szczupak. "The original intake manifold system had a variable intake with a connection valve, but that didn't give us the peak power we were looking for to meet our objectives. That was really the only major change."

Even before that first prototype engine had run, in fact, Jaguar had involved and nominated more than 80% of the production suppliers in order to ensure their commitment to the programme and their total understanding of the design and quality targets. Only world-class suppliers capable of meeting Ford's Q1 Quality Standard were selected and, once they were on board, they were fully integrated into the Simultaneous Engineering Teams (SETs). As the programme progressed more SETs were formed, until no fewer than 17 covered such areas as the cylinder block, cylinder head, engine dress systems, quality, cost, performance and refinement, with six more attending to the major manufacturing tasks. As with the design of the whole car, manufacturing personnel were involved throughout, right from the start – this was one of the positive benefits of Ford influence.

Returning to the design process, Martin Joyce elaborates upon another fundamental consideration that followed on from the debate about engine capacity and configuration.

"The next major decision concerned the number of valves per cylinder. A technical survey early in the programme determined that at least four valves per cylinder would be needed in order to achieve competitive performance. A five-valve design, with three intake and two exhaust valves, was seriously considered and tested, but we found that this offered no performance advantage.

"The resulting valve gear size was optimised for light weight, coupled with large valve sizes in order to maximise the performance. In addition to having lighter valves than any competitor engine, AJ-V8 also has the largest inlet valves in relation to bore size, thus improving its performance potential. The achievement of these two class-leading features in one engine has largely been due to the adoption of 5mm valve stems, as used in racing applications.

"The resulting twin cam design of the cylinder head was both light and simple. Clean flow paths were obtained into the chamber, which in turn was both compact and clean. The compact chamber was achieved largely through the adoption of a very narrow 'included' valve angle of 28 degrees.

"For the combustion system itself, a high compression ratio of 10.75:1 is used in combination with the

Single-cylinder test work included the assessment of a five-valve design (three intake, two exhaust), but this showed no performance advantage over four valves.

The AJ26 engine's four-valve head has the largest inlet valves in relation to bore size and the lightest valves in its class. This was achieved by copying motor racing practice and adopting 5mm valve stems.

compact, squish-free chamber. The high thermal efficiency that results from this design gives excellent power, torque and fuel consumption. The high compression ratio also helps to reduce radiated noise levels at source. This, in combination with the optimised swirl level produced by the inlet ports, results in AJ-V8 having lower combustion noise than both AJ16 and Lexus, our leading competitor.

The Engine Management System (EMS) was developed by Jaguar engineers in conjunction with Nippondenso of Japan. It helps the engine to satisfy the most stringent emissions requirements in the world, including the second phase of the Californian On-Board Diagnostics (OBDII) edict. It manages fuelling, ignition and the new electronic throttle, plus various secondary systems.

"The gas flow system of the engine was developed by a combination of computer analysis and validation test work. The Variable Cam Phasing (VCP) system is fitted to the inlet camshaft of the engine, allowing the valve timing to be optimised in two conditions. The higher airflow results in enhanced combustion quality, lower emissions and increased output. The intake and exhaust systems were tuned to complement the VCP system to give a wide spread of torque. Because the VCP boosts low and high speed torque, the long ram pipes were tuned for mid-range speeds."

A plastic intake manifold is used, for reasons of light weight, excellent thermal insulation and smooth surface finish. Advantage was also taken of this material to integrate the fuel rail into the manifold moulding, thereby reducing complexity and improving injector targeting.

The combination of these features results in impressive maximum power of 290bhp (216kW) at 6100rpm and maximum torque of 290lb ft (393Nm) at 4250rpm. These high peak values for a 4-litre unit are backed up by a very wide spread torque to give excellent driveability. Over 80% of peak torque is available from 1400rpm through to 6400rpm – virtually the full speed range of the engine. Thus the engine meets the power aspects of the design team's goal of 'Refined Power'.

"The AJ-V8 has the highest specific output in its class," states Joyce, "both in terms of power per litre and power to weight ratio. In addition the engine has the highest torque per litre value (brake mean effective pressure) in its class, both at peak torque and at high engine speeds. The achievement of high specific output was a prerequisite given our decision to adopt a relatively small displacement for our class. We match our higher displacement competitor engines for absolute performance while providing the fuel economy advantages of a smaller displacement engine."

It is tempting to judge that the engine management system (EMS), in this day and age, is one of the most important parts of the engine. But making a statement like that is rather like claiming that one wheel on a car is more important than another! Jaguar chose the Japanese company Nippondenso to supply the complete EMS very early on and it played a very important role.

Other suppliers, such as Lucas, were considered, but Lucas was very busy working with Jaguar on the vital X300 saloon car programme. Although the decision was difficult, it was felt that Lucas should remain focused totally on X300 because the success of this project was so important to Jaguar's very survival. Nippondenso, however, was another world-class supplier and demonstrated its commitment by establishing an engineering facility in Coventry. Furthermore the Japanese company was already supplying the EMS for the existing V12, and the retention of its involvement ensured continuity of technology development.

The Electronic Control Module and several major components were developed exclusively for Jaguar to meet a stringent specification based on the legal requirements in all markets, feedback from customers and the not inconsiderable experience of Jaguar itself within this field over the past 20 years.

The system was developed over a four-year period at Whitley, at Nippondenso headquarters in Japan and at the Nippondenso laboratory in Coventry. High-altitude testing was conducted at Denver, Colorado, with hot and cold testing at, respectively, Phoenix, Arizona, and Timmins, Ontario. Further data was obtained from durability running and high-speed work at Nardo in Italy and in Texas.

The fuel injection system incorporates all the features expected in a modern luxury car and the very latest technology. The many software strategies ensure that fuelling is closely controlled under all driving conditions. In order to optimise starting and transient response, the injectors are located close to the inlet valves. Although outlawed in Formula 1, traction control is available on the X100 and is achieved by electronic control of the throttle, ignition and fuelling as appropriate. The fuel injection also controls the air/fuel ratio within the very fine limits required to achieve the US emission standards, using no fewer than four oxygen sensors.

"A modern ignition system does much more than just provide sparks," according to John Corkill, who was responsible for the EMS. "Dynamic control strategies help to optimise torque, refinement, driveability and reliability. One such strategy is knock sensing. Dual block-mounted accelerometers transmit data to the Engine Control Module (ECM), where complex filtering, together with statistical data-processing algorithms, enable ignition timing to be continuously adjusted on each cylinder. The result is optimised economy and torque on all cylinders at all conditions over the life of the vehicle."

A new and exciting feature that was introduced on Formula 1 cars in the early nineties is a fly-by-wire throttle. Corkill extols its virtues. "The electronic throttle is a major step forward in technology and the throttle now includes seven functions within a single actuator. Five of these – throttling, idle speed control, cruise control, additional air for starting and emissions, and traction control – are features of most current systems, including Jaguar's. However, dynamic throttle position filtering and fine tuning of pedal progression are now features made possible by the introduction of the electronic link. They refine driveability and improve economy, allowing torque converter lock-up to be used at lower vehicle speeds. Finally the ability to integrate several systems is very important."

This fly-by-wire system means there is no direct mechanical connection between the accelerator pedal and the engine throttle.

"It gives you a number of advantages," states Crisp. "One is that it allows much more discretion in terms of throttle progression. You can achieve exactly what you want, which is very difficult with a cam cable mechanism in terms of a very gentle cracking of the throttle, and you can tailor it to give improved performance feel. The Americans may want something very different from the Europeans, but you can very easily tailor this electronically. You can also stop the driver doing things you wouldn't want him to do, such as opening the throttle too quickly. We don't do that, but it's possible.

"The real value of the fly-by-wire throttle is to improve driveability and exhaust emission control. The way in which you back off the throttle and close the throttle can be controlled – what we call 'tip in, tip out' – so you don't get jerky motion. I think there are a lot more opportunities to come and we will be exploring these as emissions legislation becomes tighter."

Previously total integration in this way was not possible. Certain functions could be controlled by the EMS but others had their own ECM, often from different suppliers. Hard-wired connections were necessary and co-ordinating the many control strategies involved was difficult. By combining all the functions within one actuator, and having the software integrated in one ECM and written by one supplier, these problems are considerably reduced. In addition, there are advantages from the durability and manufacturing points of view. No adjustments are required for any of the functions throughout the life of the car, and assembly is improved because the throttle arrives at Jaguar as a single complete unit.

Apart from controlling the primary functions, including fuelling, ignition and throttle, the ECM also manages various secondary systems including variable cam phasing, exhaust gas recirculation, fuel purging and cooling fans. The ECM has two 16-bit microprocessors with a memory capacity of 192kB and links into the vehicle electronic systems via the Controller Area Network (CAN)

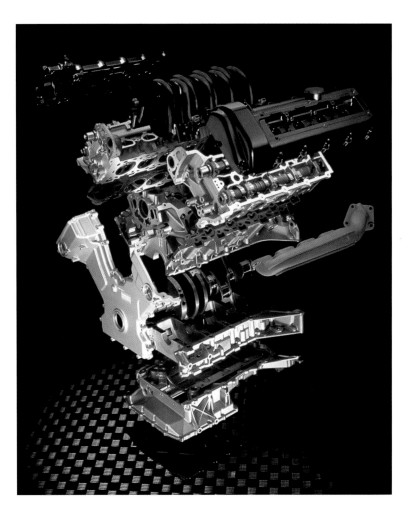

system. Engine torque can be adjusted up to 30 times per second under direct control of the Transmission Controller, in order to improve transmission shift quality. The anti-lock braking system can also request torque reduction to achieve traction control.

Emission performance is enhanced by having outstandingly fast warm-up, which is facilitated by having close-coupled catalysts and heated oxygen sensors. The catalytic converters are mounted on either bank to the exhaust manifold and begin to operate within 30 seconds of starting, significantly reducing emissions on even the shortest journeys. New catalyst coatings ensure high conversion efficiency and thermal durability.

The foundation of any engine, of course, is the block design and, guided by finite analysis, the Jaguar engineers have striven to combine light weight with structural stiffness. A cast, ribbed web linking the two banks of the engine high in the vee, combined with the closed-deck design, ensure good torsional strength for the all-aluminium block. However, the cause is considerably enhanced by the use of a structural bed plate which forms the lower half of the block. This bed plate incorporates the main bearing caps and a cast iron insert in each of the main bearing positions, providing good support for the bearings and minimising bearing clearance variation with temperature change.

The lower half of the lightweight block is formed by an aluminium alloy structural bed plate which incorporates the main bearing caps and features a cast iron insert in each of the main bearing positions. The block incorporates a cast, ribbed web which links the two banks high in the vee, contributing to a high torsional frequency of 775Hz.

the highly accurate Krebsoge powder-sintering technique. The aluminium flat-top pistons are of a short-skirt, low-friction design. The four cast iron camshafts are large in diameter for stiffness and rifle-drilled for weight reduction. The Variable Cam Phasing (VCP) system is operated on each inlet cam by an actuator and solenoids operated by the ECM. At low speeds Jaguar's VCP system increases torque by advancing the inlet cams, closing the inlet valves early. Conversely, at higher speeds the VCP achieves maximum power by retarding the inlet cams to delay valve closure.

"Fundamental to the performance of any engine," says Martin Joyce, "is its ability to draw air into the cylinders and then use it efficiently. This demands well-designed fuel, air, exhaust and combustion systems."

As mentioned earlier, the AJ-V8 is fitted with an innovative air inlet manifold, which is moulded from Polyamide composite and includes integral fuel rails for accurate location of the fuel injectors relative to the head, and for simplified assembly. The twin-spray, side-fed injectors, combined with the insulated plastic manifold, deliver outstanding hot-fuel handling, ensuring excellent starting performance.

The lubrication system is designed to operate at cornering accelerations approaching 1g. The cooled and filtered oil is channelled through a combination of cast and drilled galleries to the five main bearings, eight big-end bearings, 20 cam bearings, two VCP actuators and four chain tensioners. Ten oil drains return the oil from the heads and the chain case to the sump.

"Once early prototypes were available," recalls Szczupak, "an extensive series of statistically designed experiments, sometimes referred to as 'Taguchi experiments', were used to fully validate both the function and durability of the design. We built over 200 prototype engines in several phases."

The precision cooling system has been patented by Jaguar and consists of low-volume cylinder head and block cooling passages, end-to-end flow system layout, split-block cooling and a high-efficiency water pump. The system achieves engine warm-up in less than four minutes, reducing cold-start emissions and fuel consumption, and hastening the car's interior heating. The efficiency of the system has also allowed the capacity of the cooling system to be reduced. Szczupak elaborates the advantages of having coolant running longitudinally.

"With the help of modern analytical techniques, we have been able to optimise the flow velocities around the valves and the spark plug. With four valves per cylinder and a central spark plug, it's not an easy job to get the

The AJ26 engine has Nikasil-plated bores to reduce weight, wear and friction. Used in Grand Prix engines, Nikasil is an electroplating process which deposits a nickel-silicon carbide surface coating to a thickness of 0.003in (0.08mm).

Rather than using conventional iron liners, the bores are plated with nickel-silicon carbide (Nikasil) to a thickness of 0.003in (0.08mm). This saves 15lb (7kg) in weight and provides a highly wear-resistant, smooth surface which minimises piston friction and oil consumption. Once again Jaguar has followed Formula 1 practice in adopting this technique.

The Nikasil plating of the aluminium cylinder bores is a totally new technology for Jaguar – and indeed BMW is the only volume manufacturer using it. This meant installing a completely new plant for the plating process, and it was felt prudent to be cautious as this concept was so new. For that reason Jaguar wished to employ proven casting processes, and this persuaded the company to use low-pressure aluminium die-casting to ensure low porosity in the aluminium bore finish before plating. Clearly the quality of the aluminium bore finish has a direct relationship on the final finish of the plated bores.

"Cosworth are producing the cylinder heads," states Crisp, "and they have installed a brand-new sand-casting facility in Worcester specifically to make them. We really wanted to get very accurate positioning of the ports. We felt the Cosworth casting process was clearly the best way to go, in terms of both very accurate core positioning and overall dimensional tolerance control to reduce combustion chamber volume variability. A very accurate casting process is a key requirement."

The cylinder heads, which are again heavily ribbed for structural stiffness, to minimise radiated noise and provide a sound gasket joint, are 'handed' and offset by 18mm. As a result of the narrow, included valve angle of 28 degrees, it is possible to have a compact head size, which reduces the width of the engine.

The crankshaft, the design of which was optimised using the Cranfield 'lumped mass dynamics' model to minimise bending moments and torsional effects, is made of spheroidal graphite cast iron. Con rods are forged by water flow through and equalise all the velocities. If you start to have flow in the opposite direction, you start to have conflicting velocities and hence very variable heat transfer across the chamber. So by having it all flowing in one direction, it's much easier to even out the temperatures and then improve the ignition requirements and performance of the chamber. This is only made possible by advanced computer techniques."

The cam-drive system consists of four high-strength, single-row chains, with two chains driving the inlet cams from the crankshaft and the other two driving the exhaust cams from the inlet cams. Why choose chains, which sound like an old-fashioned solution, when belts are in more general use today?

"That's a very good question," admits Szczupak. "We spent several months trying to answer that one ourselves! We wanted a very short engine and the way we have configured the chain drive with two separate chains, you can get one of the chains to one bank within the bank offset. So the extra length of the engine is only one chain. If you have belt drive, the belt is wider for a start, and it has to go across the whole engine – so the engine becomes substantially longer. On top of that, chains are much more durable. Also you have to design the engine so that, if a chain did break, it would merely bend the valves. If one had a belt break, which happens, with this configuration it would destroy the engine. So we felt from a safety and durability aspect, as well as the package, chain were the better option. The tensioning system is very much the latest technology, not old-fashioned in any way whatsoever."

A number of key suppliers were involved by Jaguar very early on. Cosworth helped with the cylinder head design in terms of casting technology. Kolbenschmidt, the block supplier, was also involved early on. Mahle, who supply a significant number of components in Formula 1 motor racing, helped not only with the pistons but also with the bore coating. The valve manufacturer, TRW, also supplies motor racing teams. Overall, the supplier base had a strong record in pushing the frontiers of technology and using motor racing experience. Perhaps the engine even has motor racing potential?

"I hope so, as I'm quite a motor racing fan myself," says Szczupak. "But the problem at the moment is that

The lubrication system is designed to withstand cornering loads approaching 1g. Cooled and filtered oil is channelled through a combination of cast and drilled galleries to the five main bearings, eight big-end bearings, 20 cam bearings, two VCP actuators and four chain tensioners.

The water pump is mounted directly to the front of the block and discharges coolant to each bank of the engine. Split cooling of the block diverts 50% of the coolant into a gallery which bypasses the bores and delivers the flow to the cylinder heads at the rear of the engine. Here it mixes with the other 50% used to cool the bores. The system has been patented by Jaguar.

there isn't an obvious category for Jaguar to race in. Certainly the structural strength and lightness of the engine means there's nothing to stop us using it if a suitable formula was available. We have no plans at the moment, but that's not to say we couldn't. And we could see some exciting performance versions of the engine in the future..."

Very clearly, cliché though it is, this fabulous V8 engine is history in the making. We are witnessing the birth of a worthy successor to the brilliant Jaguar XK and V12 engines of the past, not forgetting the present AJ16.

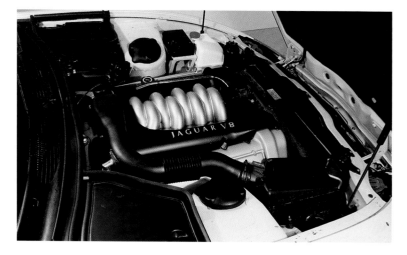

Today underbody style is important and gone are engine bays – such as on the early fuel-injected XJS – that resemble a plumber's nightmare of visible pipework and wiring. Stylists were briefed to suggest several approaches, and here we see two that were not adopted.

To the great names – such as Heynes, Hassan, Baily and Mundy – we must now add Crisp, Szczupak, Reddington, Cooke, Massey, Joyce and a host of other gifted engineers. The list of contributors is longer than in the old days because the challenge becomes ever tougher, as Szczupak points out.

"Designing a new engine through a deep recession isn't an easy thing to do! We have spent $240 million on the engine alone. That is the total programme cost and includes all the facilities at Bridgend, all vendor tooling, all engineering costs and all launch costs. We've actually spent just less than budget, and we've delivered on 'piece' cost. So the engine has met the performance and financial targets."

Jaguar has a long tradition of launching new engines in sports cars, then extending their use to mainstream saloons. The XK was installed in the XK120 to try it out on a more tolerant bunch of enthusiast owners before unleashing it on saloon car customers – how times have changed! The V12 was put in the ageing E-type in an effort to revive that great car, and again to prove the new power unit. And the AJ6 was launched in the XJS. Szczupak is interested to be reminded of this tradition.

"At one time Ford said, 'thou shalt never launch a new engine and new car simultaneously', but here we

are doing just that! The X100 was the first new car to come along. To get the best out of a package, you really have to design an engine and a car in 'sync'. If we had designed the X100 to take the AJ16 engine, we wouldn't have had the package benefits of the AJ26 being a foot shorter than the AJ16. So that gave Bob Dover's team huge freedom in terms of style. So we concluded that you have to do a new engine and a new car together – anything else will always be a compromise.

"So the question then was, would we put it in the saloon car first and then in the sports car, or vice versa? The advantage of putting it in the sports car first is that it gives you what we call low-volume ramp. So it was a conscious decision to put it in the sports car first, as a low-volume ramp to bring the manufacturing efficiency up. If we'd tried to launch the engine with a big bang in high volume, it would have put a huge burden on the manufacturing people to get up to speed quickly with a completely new facility.

"So if you do launch in a sports car, you achieve quality from Job 1. You then devote effort to building up manufacturing efficiency without any risk to quality. That was the philosophy behind putting it in the X100."

While Trevor Crisp's role has been to oversee the whole powertrain, David Szczupak's has been to mastermind the AJ-V8 engine. Although he is keen to stress that this was a team effort, he offers some observations when asked to define his role.

"My biggest contribution was to make sure that the team worked together with agreed goals and discipline, and to deliver things on time. Part of all this was trying to use data to drive us, using benchmarking, and understanding where we'd reached. What are the unknowns? How do we get data to make informed decisions rather than go on gut reactions? Questioning things and avoiding the 'we've always done it that way' mentality to try to optimise the solutions. Trying to guide a team that consisted of a very strong technical and highly intellectual group of individuals, people with PhDs and Masters' degrees, as well as the guys who started their careers as apprentices and have years of experience in high-performance engine design.

"I think the important thing for a powertrain guy to understand is that we don't sell engines on their own – we sell cars. At the end of the day, it's all about making a product that you're proud of. I think the good thing about working on the X100 programme is that it's a really exciting car.

"When I drove the very early prototypes that obviously had all the problems, I started to get a little nervous and worried about it. But the cars I've driven close to launch, the VP prototypes, really do feel superb. I get a great thrill out of driving the car, not just from the engine and the performance, but also from the steering, the handling, the brakes, the whole package. I think the look of the car and the actual driving experience complement each other superbly."

Trevor Crisp is also pleased with his team, and enormously proud of the finished result.

"We set our objective of being best in class for performance, and that meant aiming at BMW. Lexus was clearly the leader in terms of refinement and so we set our sights on that. We did a great deal of benchmarking of all the major systems in the car in terms of where we wanted to set our objectives.

"I think we really have achieved all of those objectives. Performance is up on the original target – and our engine is more powerful than the 4-litre BMW V8. It's on a par with Lexus in terms of noise levels, and that's quite an achievement remembering that noise rises with power output – and our engine is significantly more powerful than the Lexus V8.

It is appropriate that David Szczupak should have the last word on what he and his team have achieved with the exciting new AJ-V8 engine, which in the future may appear in saloon models as well.

"To sum up the best in class features: specific power output of 72.5bhp or 54kW per litre; highest torque per litre, both at 1500rpm and at peak torque; the lightest engine in class at just over 440lb, some 90lb lighter than the AJ16 engine; highest power-to-weight and power-to-volume ratios in class, giving a very strong and small package for the power output; stiffest powertrain; lightest valve gear in class, with a single valve assembly weighing just under 3½oz; precision cooling, to enable us to have the engine fully warm in under four minutes; lowest friction levels and lowest service costs in class.

"The guys working on the engine were there to create an excellent motor car, not just an excellent engine in isolation. Our job is all about making cars that are exciting to drive."

As the June 1996 launch of the engine approached, the internal designation of AJ26 was succeeded by the public name of AJ-V8. By any name and any standards the new engine is a superlative example of state-of-the-art engineering.

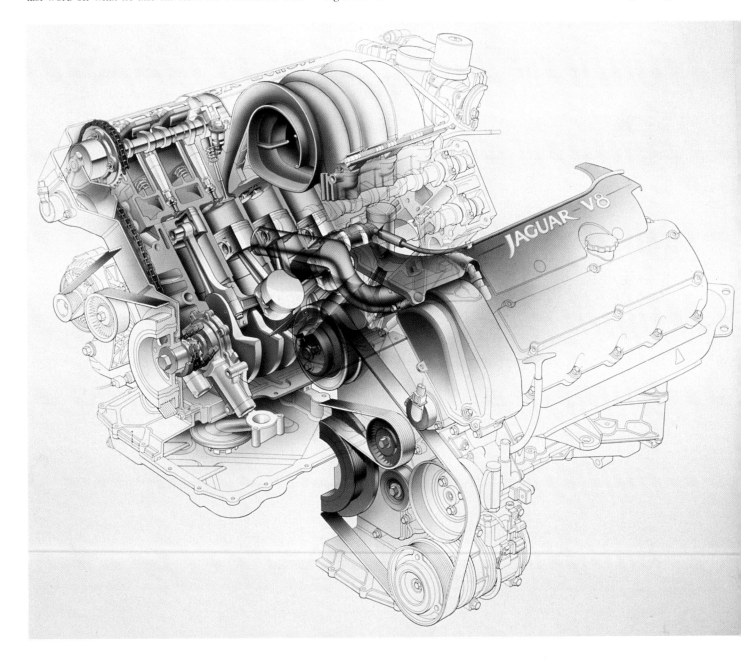

THE FIRST 'REAL' PROTOTYPES EMERGE – 1994

The hero of the hour, MP19, which had played a crucial role in securing Programme Approval. It had starred in the video, although it was then red and looked rather smarter. Ian Minards is seen with it.

There was intense relief at the start of 1994. Jaguar was still in business and the X100 programme had finally been approved. However, this was not a time to relax as many hurdles still needed to be overcome, although most of these now related directly to the car itself. Indeed the pressure was on to turn the concept into reality in a time scale that was now very short, even by Japanese standards.

Meanwhile, the search for the spy photographer who had supplied *Car* magazine with shots of the car had been followed up by Security. It was discovered that they had been taken in the Styling studio and, due to the level of detailing, it was possible to fix the date. There was also a distorted reflection of the rogue in a turned aluminium gear lever knob. Suspicion fell on a particular individual but, to Bob Dover's disappointment, there was a reluctance to bring in the police and expose the traitor.

In January the No Adjust Car Build team gave a presentation to the X100 group. This concept, which had been applied on the Mustang, is explained by Kevin Riches, another key member of the Project Team, with responsibilities for body-in-white and trim engineering.

"The principle of No Adjust Car Build is that you have two master jigging location holes, and everything on the body-in-white is jigged to these. Then you have secondary locators, and everything is dimensioned from the two master jigging location holes to these secondary locators. We have also used these same holes as interior trim locators."

These primary and secondary locators are effectively datum points from which all panel dimensions can be checked very accurately to ensure that they, and thus the sum of the parts, are within much tighter tolerances than was traditionally the case. As any restorer of XKs or E-types will know, bodies from the same model used to vary by as much as an inch in places.

"The Jaguars of the distant past," comments Paul Walker, "would have been designed with what I would call Total Adjust Car Build, which means you slot everything together in every direction, lead-load it on the assembly line, equip the man on the line with a mallet, and give him fixings that he can adjust with shims, packing pieces and so on. This required an advanced level of skill, involved considerable time per car, and created a high degree of variability with no two cars the same – no consistency of quality and a poor result. We've changed radically in our approach by engineering quality into the car from the very beginning, and I think it shows."

A computer aid developed by Concentra, who are based at the University of Warwick Science Park, significantly reduces design time and was used on the X100 project. Known as Knowledge Based Engineering (KBE), it can, for example, be used to automate and accelerate the design of panel reinforcement structures. Eleven different bonnet reinforcement panels were designed in this way with the result that a fully surfaced panel was translated into a fully pressable, detailed design – and all within one and a half hours!

"Basically we gave the system a set of rules saying we need a bonnet of certain stiffness and certain overall dimensions," states Riches. "With just a few simple rules like that laid down, the system will actually generate the geometries for you. We used it to create, for example, all the wheel envelopes for X100 to give the wheelarch clearances, having asked our chassis colleagues to put in some rules of thumb for vertical and longitudinal displacements. Care was required, however, because X100 is a sports car and the XJS was a grand tourer, so a long-time XJS owner moving on to an XK8 will expect the same level of ride refinement. For that you need fore and aft compliance, wheel travel, and so on. Generating the correct wheel envelopes with KBE saved a great deal of time."

KBE was also used for designing hinges, wiper system legislation checks, lamp feasibility and instrument visibility assessments. Jaguar's success in implementing automated and truly concurrent engineering is recognised as unequalled in the automotive industry.

The individual who represented Purchasing on the Project Team was David Williams, who takes up the story. "Programme approval was a crucial stage because it meant we could initiate our long-lead tooling funds. It was absolutely essential to move on to some production tooling at this point because we were so far behind schedule. We had planned to do this in April 1993, but the X100 programme had not been signed off at this stage – and this was also the period when we went through the paring of capital expenditure. Our plans were also delayed while we studied the possibility of building the car in Portugal. Because of these delays, we now had a timing crisis to overcome.

"So obtaining that approval for X100 was critical to maintaining Programme Timing. We kicked off our major suppliers in December 1993 and January 1994. Actually, it's quite amazing how difficult it is to spend money

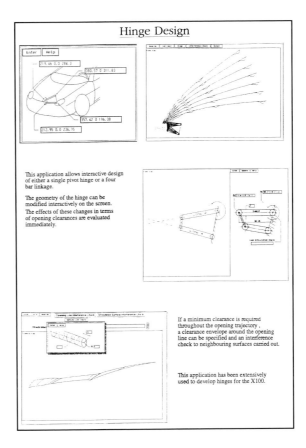

Hinge Design

This application allows interactive design of either a single pivot hinge or a four bar linkage.

The geometry of the hinge can be modified interactively on the screen. The effects of these changes in terms of opening clearances are evaluated immediately.

If a minimum clearance is required throughout the opening trajectory, a clearance envelope around the opening line can be specified and an interference check to neighbouring surfaces carried out.

This application has been extensively used to develop hinges for the X100.

Computers were used extensively in X100 design work. The concept of Knowledge Based Engineering was used, for example, to develop hinges.

when it actually becomes available and when you've starved suppliers of funds and kept them going on a thread. There was quite a bit of inertia."

Remembering that the challenge was not merely to produce a superb new car but also radically to improve the entire business, Jim Padilla exudes enthusiasm on one of his pet subjects.

"One of the most important things we did on improving quality at Jaguar was achieving the Ford Q1 rating – a difficult chore. The initial assessments the guys put together said, 'Q1? We'll do it after we launch X300'. My response was, 'No way. We're going to do it six months before we launch X300. We need the quality system in place before you get the new product'. I'm really proud of the fact that each of the plants took up the challenge – and they really ripped up the old approach.

A comparatively small number of prototypes had to work very hard, and MP19 could not rest on its laurels. Unlike the other Mechanical Prototypes, it had a crude representation of the final interior and was used extensively for air conditioning test work.

Styling staff refining details on an X100 Convertible.

"The advantage of Q1 is simple. It moves the quality initiative from the plant manager's office to the shop floor. It propels customer feedback and data to the people who can do something about it. Nobody knows our cars better than the people who are putting them together a hundred, even two hundred, times a day. The difficulty we had was that generally we didn't know what out problems were and, when we did, we didn't tell the right people what the hell was going on, and ask them how to fix it.

"What we have now is an energised system where the customer data goes to the shop floor first. The people on the shop floor translate the data into the way they do their jobs, and into statistical process control techniques whereby they know what they're producing. They know if they're in control and capable, or if they're out of control. And they have reaction plans at the hourly level. The responsibility doesn't lie with the supervisor, the superintendent, the quality control manager or the plant manager, because they're not there all the time – it's up to the hourly-paid operator. And that's what really pleases me."

David Hudson, the Plant Director, takes up the thread. "We started taking our hourly-paid teams to Bob Dover's project meetings. They would tell the team of engineers, 'This is what we've learned about these parts of the car: we're happy about building this, but not that'. This wasn't management talking to Bob's group, but the men and women who do it every day."

Bob Dover is particularly keen on the old C-type sports racers. "For a few weeks we had been discussing a car we had coded X100-C. The idea was to parallel the introduction of the C-type, 45 years prior to our 1996 launch, with a lightweight structure and simple body on the X100 mechanicals, in the same way as the C-type was related to the XK120.

"I had several discussions with Frank Marsden and Manfred Lampe. Clearly there was no Engineering money for such a venture, but the three of us started to do some detailed schemes. The target was to use the Detroit Show in January 1995 to display the car to drum up interest in the marketplace, to reinforce our credibility in the sports car sector and to enhance the Jaguar image following the launch of the X300 the previous autumn. Frank came up with a terrific concept for using a sandwich construction akin to the XJ220. I discussed it with Stephen Perrin, our Marketing Director, and Mike Dale, both of whom were very enthusiastic.

"We also started negotiations with potential suppliers of model cars. I intended to register the design so that we could attract royalty payments. John Maries organised a meeting with the Chairman and General Manager of Maisto, respectively Mr and Mrs Ngan. When we asked whether a 1/12, 1/18 or 1/24 model was appropriate, Mr Ngan said, 'All of them!'. He was very keen to proceed."

In March Bob Dover took his troops on a two-day team-building course with Sporting Bodymind at Studley. The experience yielded many unrepeatable stories. A chance meeting in the bar on the last night with a group from Rover inspired the X100 Project Team to write a song to compete with that composed by their rivals. It would be kinder to spare the reader even an extract...

Returning to the X100 story, a 'Mission Statement' had been created as an encapsulation of what the Project Team felt the new car should be. It ran as follows: 'An exciting, elegant and refined luxury sports car with effortless performance. The X100 is a luxury sports car for people who enjoy driving and appreciate refinement.

Harking back to the days when, in 1950-51, Jaguar developed the XK120 into the racing C-type, thought was given to building a spritual successor. The X100C was conceived as a stripped, shortened and lightened version to be built in very limited numbers.

Refined power coupled with an adaptive five-speed transmission ensures performance. Interior appointments are stylish and aesthetically satisfying without unnecessary gadgetry or ostentation. The exterior style refreshes and re-states the classic Jaguar themes. Its features reflect a single-minded dedication to practicality and excellence of execution.'

"If you look at the chassis," states Paul Walker, "it's completely new for X100 front and rear. The XJS rear suspension stems back to 1961 and the E-type, with the twin coil spring rear and radius rods. So with X100 we set out to achieve a distinct improvement in the chassis dynamics, and we recognised that we couldn't do that by just re-tuning the existing XJS suspensions.

"So we took the decision to do a developed version of the X300 rear suspension because the biggest attribute it has, apart from commonality, is anti-squat, which the XJS lacks and has always suffered from. Therefore it has always been necessary to trade spring rates and pitch rates to try to overcome that, and make the car stiffer."

"When we were developing the X300," states Ken Heap, "we found that the torque of the supercharged car gave us a few suspension problems, particularly in controlling rear axle tramp. So we created a much stiffer rear mounting frame that we call the mono-strut. When we

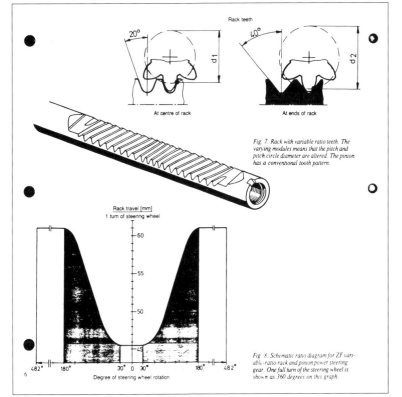

Fig. 7: Rack with variable ratio teeth. The varying modules means that the pitch and pitch circle diameter are altered. The pinion has a conventional tooth pattern.

Fig. 8: Schematic ratio diagram for ZF variable-ratio rack and pinion power steering gear. One full turn of the steering wheel is shown as 360 degrees on this graph.

An innovation for the rack and pinion steering system gives variable ratio. As the steering is turned, the conventional pinion meshes with rack teeth whose angle and spacing progressively increase, lowering the ratio and making the steering more direct.

built an X100 prototype with the V8, which has such a high level of torque, the mono-strut was found to be beneficial for not only controlling this torque but also for improving body refinement."

"The rear axle has been completely redesigned for this car," Trevor Crisp points out. "We've gone to an on-centre diff rather than have the propshaft offset to the crown wheel and pinion. This ensures that we have a

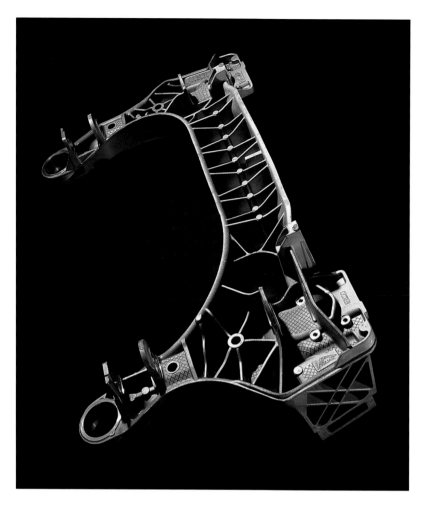

The cast aluminium front axle beam, normally a mundane component, is raised almost to a computer-designed art form. Its aesthetic appeal is reminiscent of pre-war Bugatti front axles.

crisp, precise car to handle. So we decided to take the steering changes we'd made for X300, with the variable speed assistance, and add to that variable ratio, so that we could improve the turning circle, the manoeuvrability of the car, and the steering precision and feel – but not make the car too 'darty' at high speeds. So we have used the variable ratio to achieve that.

"The die-cast aluminium front suspension beam was produced from start to finish as a CAD/CAM project. A lot of analysis work was done on the design before any parts were produced, and this is the first time a Jaguar beam hasn't needed development for structural reasons. It has gone straight from concept design to production.

"We took the first sand-cast prototype and put it through the pothole braking test, which is our most stringent structural test for the front beam, and it passed unscathed. We have never, ever achieved that. We had troubles on the Series III XJ saloon with

totally aligned propshaft with no significant angularity on any of the joints, in the interests of refinement."

"We wanted to show similar, or even better, steering improvements than we'd achieved on X300 over XJ40," continues Paul Walker. "We wanted to make X100 a

pothole braking and beam deflections. We didn't achieve it straight away on XJ40. We had problems for XJ81, when we put the 6-litre V12 into the XJ40. I think this is a fine example of how the technology has progressed."

By March Dover had found ways to fund the new C-

Most of the Mechanical Prototypes were XJS lookalikes, but under the skin they were very different. Fitted with the new V8 engine, X100 front and rear suspensions, and various other new developments, they allowed vital testing to be conducted in anonymity.

type, but Nick Scheele was not keen on the idea and it was shelved. He was concerned that the car might overshadow the launch of the important long-wheelbase saloon. In April a Ford Probe seat was tried in an X100 but it was too tight, which meant having to find £2.5 million for a new height-rise seat mechanism. At the end of the month, Alex Trotman gave a presentation on the major reorganisation involved in the 'Ford 2000' concept.

"Shortly after Ford 2000 we had our first visits from some senior Ford Vice Presidents who had not previously been to Jaguar," recalls Paul Walker. "One was Dave Gorman, who was in charge of world-wide manufacturing for Ford, and he attended a X100 Launch Review. My Principal Engineer in charge of suspension design held up the front beam and said, 'Now, wouldn't it be a privilege to be run over by that?'.

"There was a hushed silence round the room while everyone looked at Gorman to see whether his sense of humour would run to this rather unusual comment on our design expertise. Fortunately, it did!"

Although the F-type, or XJ41, never saw light of day, certain benefits have been passed down, according to Walker. "Alan Ancliffe, who died from cancer at an early age in November 1994, had been very heavily involved in the XJ41 project and he ran our CAD packaging and vehicle CAE analysis group. Alan was responsible for a lot of the procedures that X100 has benefited from, and all the early package work on X100, and the lessons learned from XJ41. Sadly he never saw the results of his labours with X100, but he did a lot to establish that department."

Ian Minards takes up the prototype story again. "As we finished the Simulator build, we were planning to move on to the Mechanical Prototypes – the MPs – and already doing packaging work for them. These were running vehicles which looked like XJSs, but had X100 suspensions and AJ26 engines. They were purpose-built bodyshells rather than modified existing cars, and all were constructed at our Castle Bromwich plant in the Experimental Body-in-White shop.

"Twenty-seven MPs were built and they were all

black, apart from one PASCAR (see the '1996' chapter) car that was white. You couldn't tell them apart from a standard XJS, unless you knew where to look – they had special bonnet pins! It was a great form of disguise. They were built from October 1993 to February 1994.

"We also built five crash MPs. They were funny cars to look at because, to save precious development funds, they were hybrids with one side X100 and the other side XJS – they were for side impact work. Another five cars were front crash simulators and just rolling shells. Then there were six cars called Sensor Calibration MPs, which

had more of a representative front end structure and were used for calibrating the air bag sensors. They were crashed at a variety of speeds to ensure that the sensors didn't go off in a very low-speed impact, but did in a high-speed one."

Several MPs were put to work in North America, doing cold weather testing at Timmins, Ontario, and then

This car, which the author drove during the preparation of this book, was used for developing the Engine Management System. Of the other 26 MPs, six were used for airbag calibration, two for ride and handling development and no fewer than ten for front and side crash testing.

MP29 was rear crash tested, but not intentionally! Its usefulness ended when it was struck by a Ford truck during hot climate testing in Phoenix, Arizona.

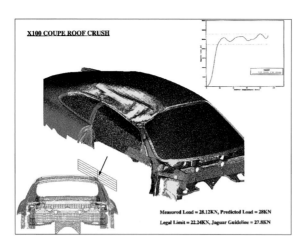

X100 COUPE ROOF CRUSH

Measured Load = 28.12KN, Predicted Load = 28KN
Legal Limit = 22.24KN, Jaguar Guideline = 27.8KN

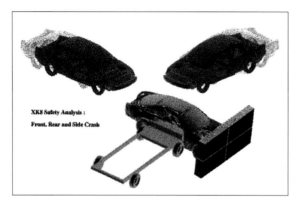

XK8 Safety Analysis :
Front, Rear and Side Crash

With constraints on the budget, it was important to simulate crash testing on computer as much as possible rather than destroy prototypes that could be employed more usefully on other work.

A variety of angles of impact can be assessed on computer, including, presumably, what happens when hit up the rear by a Ford truck!

experiencing the other extreme at Phoenix, Arizona. The working life of one was terminated in Arizona when a truck crashed into the back of it. The truck happened to be a Ford...

The rubber seals were another important aspect of X100 development. Jaguar has always prided itself on producing highly refined cars and a convertible is inevitably a particular challenge. How the XJS Convertible had developed, many years after the coupé, was the complete antithesis of the ideal approach. The two versions of the XJS were totally different animals that did not even share windscreen angles, and the seals, according to Paul Heynes, had evolved rather than been designed. He and his colleagues were determined to make a quantum leap forward. They began by writing a description of all the XJS's deficiencies and the pitfalls that had to be avoided in their clean-sheet-of-paper approach to X100.

"We had a significant input to the design of the sheet metal about where we wanted to put the seals," states Heynes. "If you have a difficult route for a seal, it becomes complicated and requires mouldings. Distortions can occur and these affect sealing performance. So now we design the sealing faces more specifically to suit the seals. The considerations include swing angles and compliance, so that we achieve the right quality and refinement for door closure."

The Nishikawa engineers, whom Stokes and Dover had visited several months before, were superb partners

in all the design detail. There were some initial hurdles in developing the relationship, particularly with the language barrier, but Heynes judges that Nishikawa did an outstanding job.

"Right from the outset we made sure we considered all of our customers," Heynes continues, "and when we say customers we include Manufacturing Assembly. If you make something difficult to fit on the production line, it's more likely to be done wrong and takes longer. We also had to reduce the cost of the seals to be more competitive, which means fewer parts. That has made a significant contribution compared with the XJS, and assembling all the seals and related components now takes less than half the time it used to.

"Another aspect of sealing that we tried to improve was overall refinement levels in the car. It's not just about sealing the windows. It's about sealing the complete body – noise through the structure, road noise and wind noise. Throughout this programme we've been using an acoustic wind tunnel, taking each prototype stage of the car there to obtain very definitive, objective measurements. We can remove powertrain and tyre noise, and focus on specific areas of the car. This is difficult to do on a test track: you can't hang out of the side with microphones!"

An acoustic wind tunnel is similar to a dynamic wind tunnel, but operates in a semi-acoustic chamber. Wind speed and direction can be controlled, and some yaw angle can be applied to the car if required. Smoke and other visual aids can also be used to assist. For this work, all the body joints and openings are blanked off with tape.

"We then do what we call 'windowing'," continues Heynes. "We can remove a small piece of tape and, with a microphone inside the car, assess whatever leakage noise or transmission noise comes through that area. It could be part of a seal, part of a window frame, a form feature, a mirror, a bonnet line.

"This method identifies the areas for improvement. We assess each area to see whether the noise is caused by air turbulence around the body, or whether there's actually a leak path. A leak is the most obvious problem, and curing it is a matter of addressing body joints, or plugging holes, or altering the shape, or trying a new moulding on a seal."

'Active Glass' – or 'Automatic Dropping Glass' – is fitted on both the Coupé and Convertible. With a convertible in particular, it can be

difficult to control the soft-top form accurately enough to achieve the necessary levels of seal contact refinement on the edge of the glass. The seal on X100, therefore, is like a conventional glass window channel: the glass drops slightly to disengage from the channel when you open the door, then automatically rises and locks itself back into the channel when you close the door. As well as providing an additional extension of glass into the seal, this system also creates a positive locking feature and contains the normal aerodynamic effect that pulls the glass outwards at higher speeds.

"The door seals looked frighteningly expensive when Bob Dover and I went over to visit Nishikawa," reflects Paul Stokes. "But the prototypes that arrived were of better quality than our normal production source – they were magnificent. When the XK8 becomes available, the door seals are, I think, something that automotive people will comment about."

Mike Beasley has a story about seals that amuses him considerably. Perhaps it should be added that the 'victim' was not Paul Heynes...

"In the early days, when we realised we had to test cars far more aggressively for water leaks, we enjoyed immensely the idea that the engineer who designed the boot seal should actually sit in the boot as the car went through the water leak test. To his credit, the young engineer turned up at 7.30 one morning and did his duty. I think he probably learned a lot about sealing cars that morning!"

After consideration of several electrical system proposals that would include carry-over modules from the XJS, the system gradually became more customised to X100, as a result of being driven by added features, marketing requirements and styling. An important feature is multiplexing, which replaces most of the wiring 'spaghetti' of a conventional harness with simplified wiring and five localised, networked, intelligent control modules.

"Multiplexing was relatively new at the beginning of the project and is a major advance," states Liam Brown of Electrical Engineering. "It was chosen because it reduces the number of wires and connections in the car, saving weight and space. We have a tremendous level of electrical features in this car, yet we were given a smaller package space. There's simply no way we could have manufactured the car with traditional harness methods."

There was also a requirement from Manufacturing to cut down the time it takes to build the car, and multiplexing makes a significant contribution to that – assembling the electrical systems of X100 takes two hours less than the XJS installation. The reduced number of wires is not the only reason, however, for some assemblies are now built by sub-contractors.

"We first looked at the overall electrical layout on CAD," continues Brown. "We were able to create 3D

Considerable work was carried out in acoustic wind tunnels. A process called 'windowing' involves taping over all apertures, then removing sections to measure noise.

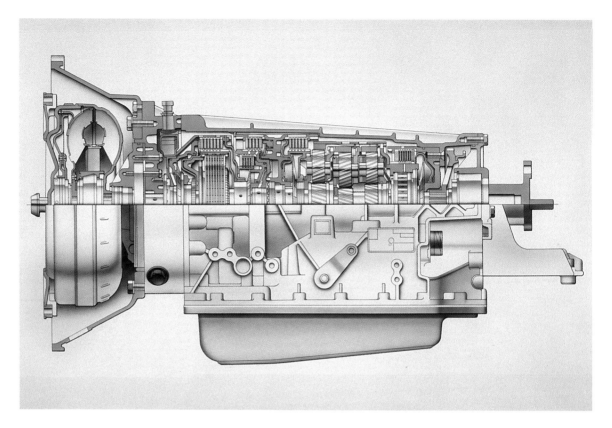

models on the CAD for the first time, and we routed the wiring through all the body-in-white and trim areas. Wires, clips, connectors – everything is pictorially drawn on the system. That was a major step forward from the X300.

"We have also progressed tremendously with CAE, using it to diagnose and check out each of the systems. The considerable CAE work we did very early in the programme avoided many potential problems.

For example, we now have an extremely refined module which sees very low current – 10 milli-amps and below in some cases. With the door windows, say, we could have a situation where the glass goes down properly on one side because the volt drop is right, but operates hesitantly on the other side because there might be three times the length of wire, giving a greater volt drop due to the resistance in the wire. As a result of looking at the architecture and calculating Ohms Law, using electronic systems, FMEA tools and suchlike, we've been able to make any changes early on in the programme. Previously we wouldn't have seen a problem until we had a car off production, and then we would have had to go and physically test the car to eliminate it."

Meanwhile, during April and May, two very expensive prototypes – a Coupé and a Convertible – were built by hand. These Special Mechanical Prototypes (SMPs) were steel X100 lookalikes made from prototype tooling. They were used for checking feasibility, aerodynamic work, cooling, any major sealing issues, body joints, torsional rigidity and NVH (Noise, Vibration and Harshness).

"The SMPs were built," states Keith Adams, "to give confidence to committing to the body-in-white sheet metal production tooling, but only after considerable debate in the Project Team 'War Room'."

In parallel with all the design and development work on the new V8 engine, the important matter of the transmission unit was being discussed, designed, built and developed in conjunction with the engine and the various levels of prototype. It may be regretted by some, including myself, that there is to be no manual gearbox offered, but the lack of demand demolishes any argument in support of a manual, even for a sports car. The 'J' gate selector fitted to the saloons and the X100 does, admittedly, give a good degree of control.

"The gearbox is brand new," says Trevor Crisp. "The project was started with ZF right from the very concept stage of the engine. Although other manufacturers will be using the gearbox, it was designed specifically with our needs and specifications in mind. We laid down what we needed in the way of features, but the design and development were ZF's responsibility.

"It was essential, we believed, to have a five-speed for both performance and economy. If there's one criticism that most Americans would make of most European cars, it's the lack of initial performance feel. Generally in Europe we are oriented towards high power outputs, whereas in America they are more interested in very rapid launch performance, due to the short ramps on to freeways and suchlike. That has been criticism of many European engines in the US, and that arises largely from their choice of gear ratios and the way they tune their engines to give torque at low speeds. So we felt that we really needed a lower first gear and a very high overdrive gear for cruising. To obtain the spread of ratios, you therefore need five gears.

"Benchmarking of all the rival transmissions was carried out to establish our objectives. We thought that the Lexus had about the best shift quality, so we set ZF the task of at least equalling that."

Keith Turfrey has led the transmission development on behalf of Jaguar and liaised with ZF. "To match the transmission to the power unit, a new, low-inertia torque converter has been chosen for the best performance. A new feature is the controlled-slip lock-up clutch that replaces the normal fixed lock-up and anti-vibration damper. This electronically-controlled feature gives partial lock-up in high gears at low speeds to give refinement over a wide speed range and enhanced economy."

Additionally a new electronic gearshift controller has been developed to provide optimum performance. This high-capacity, high-speed, 32-bit unit controls the three solenoid valves used for gear selection and lock-up control, and the combination of five pressure regulator valves gives precise control of the individual clutch pressure through a shift.

As if designing and developing a new sports car were not enough, another problem reared its head during the year. Jaguar had been used to being at the mercy of Dollar/Sterling fluctuations, but now other currencies entered the equation. One disadvantage of dealing with companies situated all around the world is the risk of massive currency variations, either as a result of the movement of Sterling or the local currency.

"Both the Yen and the Deutschmark have been difficult to handle," says Paul Stokes. "But the companies we have been dealing with sat down and thought through our problem. They realised they had to find better ways of doing their business with us, otherwise we would have to leave them in the longer term.

"Currency fluctuations were at their most severe at a very critical point in the programme. But there was no way we could abandon, say, an engine management system halfway through the project and, with tail between legs, find another supplier to pick it up. Our timing would have gone out of the window.

"Bob Dover and I had a couple of overseas trips when it was pretty important we came back with the right agreement – we could see our costs zipping away. They were pretty draining sessions, the meetings sometimes lasting as long as 10 hours – and these companies didn't seem to have air conditioning in their offices.

"Nippondenso again showed exceptionally good

The glass-fibre styling models were still being used during 1994 to verify details. A red bonnet badge was considered, and originally it was intended to have a grey splitter bar with Sport trim cars and a chromed one with Classic trim. Later it was agreed they all be chrome, as on the E-type.

HM The Queen and the Duke of Edinburgh were given a private glimpse of the secret new sports cars when they visited the factory in 1994. Prince Philip is seen with Bob Dover (centre) and Mike Beasley (left), the Queen with Jaguar Chairman Nick Scheele.

behaviour. They recognised our problem, and we, of course also recognised that it wasn't of their making. So we sat down and examined where, in the longer term, certain components could be manufactured. As a result Nippondenso now has a super facility in Telford, Shropshire, where they make air conditioning systems for Jaguar and Rover.

"With Ogihara we signed a very large contract in Sterling. Here we were faced with a Japanese company trying to raise the price to claw back on the exchange rate. But they needed Sterling and we were able to reach an agreement with them – and they now have people working in the UK as well. Again, we developed an exceptionally good relationship with Ogihara – their local authority in Japan made an award to Jaguar for putting work into the district.

"Although they work with Mercedes-Benz and BMW, and lots of other manufacturers, many of our suppliers always seem to have a twinkle in their eye when they're dealing with Jaguar. I'm sure in many cases our volumes don't produce large profits, but companies seem to like being associated with Jaguar."

On 15 September Padilla, Ennos and Dover travelled to Ford's proving ground at Dunton for a 'ride and drive' assessment of competitor cars. They arrived early and sat down for lunch in the usual place, but then realised with

horror that they were eating the Ford Directors' lunch. They hurriedly moved to the tent outside where their sandwiches were laid out! A day later the Jaguar men were given a standing ovation by their Ford colleagues, led by Jac Nasser. This was based on early feedback about the X300 saloon, due to be launched a fortnight later, and was apparently unheard of in Ford circles.

The next prototype stage was the construction of Evaluation Prototypes (EPs), cars that look like the real thing but still contain some parts off prototype tooling. Build was due to begin in October 1994, and the schedule was only just met after a serious hitch occurred. Mark White explains.

"About a month before delivery of the EP sub-assemblies was due, the prototype panels weren't ready. This meant that Bob Dover, myself, Phil Hodgkinson, Keith Adams and Kevin Richardson all worked virtually day and night at the local prototype panel supplier for two or three months. I remember one occasion when I was still there at 1.00am trying to get parts finished for delivery into Castle Bromwich at 7.00am for the day's work there.

"We ran double shifts and triple shifts. Whatever happened, we were going to meet our programme date. The body-in-white team and the Jaguar team weren't going to let a little thing like having no tools and no panels stand in the way of delivering a bodyshell to Track 7 at Browns

In late 1994 the first of the Evaluation Prototypes was completed. These cars, which looked like the real thing, were largely built off prototype tooling but were the first to be assembled on a production line basis.

Lane. Bob Dover literally manned all the major meetings and put his foot down where necessary.

"That really moved the project away from our supplier to our in-house facility at Castle Bromwich, where we had to say to our small prototype shop, 'By the way, how do you fancy making all the EPs for us from scratch?' They were always going to carry out the major assembly work, but they weren't supposed to be doing any of the sub-assemblies. In the end they built all of the EPs largely from scratch, with some pretty heavyweight jigging to ensure dimensional conformity."

During the middle of EP build, on 8 December, HM The Queen and Prince Philip visited Browns Lane. Following formalities in the museum, the party moved into another room for luncheon, all, that is, apart from Her Majesty and the Duke. Only then were the dust sheets removed from two cars tucked away in the corner, revealing Coupé and Convertible versions of X100...

"Apart from the two hand-built SMPs, the EPs were the first cars that looked like real X100s," says Ian Minards, who was responsible for the construction of all prototype cars. "One of the key processes we put in was called Green List. This was a meeting held every morning between myself, Russ Varney from the Vehicle Office, Dave Williams from Purchase, and Martin Bazeley and Alan Jordan from Finance. Every morning the designers brought their releases to us and we vetted them for cost, weight and purchase lead times and accuracy.

"We built the EPs at Browns Lane on Track 7, a mini track that emulates the main track in Assembly. EP8, the first car completed, was a Coupé started in October and it took only four weeks to build. This is probably the quickest Jaguar has ever put together an initial prototype – in the old days it used to take months to build the first one. We were delighted. The second car, EP33, the first Convertible, took only 11 days.

"But we didn't do everything quite right! We got EP8 to the end of the track and came to start it up – and it wouldn't start! Initially we found the starter motor was connected the wrong way round. Then we found the fuel pump didn't work and the ignition amplifiers weren't wired correctly. So we had three minor problems – no crank, no fuel and no spark!

"It was about 8.00pm when the car finally started. I had the honour of driving it off the track. I was a little bit 'chicken' because I had to drive the car onto a ramp for some checks at the end of the track, so I first put it in reverse to check the brakes. They were fine, so I drove off the end of the track, back down the length of the track and onto the ramp.

"There was a round of applause. It was a very big day for everybody."

REFINING THE FINAL DETAILS – 1995

MP19, the star of stage and screen, was the first lookalike car to be made into a runner and needed disguise. It was important, however, not to change the airflow to the mouth or the screen base because the car was to be used for air conditioning development.

This was to be the last full calendar year for the X100 project, as launch was a mere 21 months away at the start of 1995. With such a short overall time scale, the action had been frenetic from the very beginning. Now the project took on a new level of excitement as the latest prototypes looked like finished cars, not that anyone outside Jaguar would have known it.

"After MP19's starring role in 1993 in the video," recalls Ian Minards, "the car went to Canada to do its air conditioning work. So we had to come up with a form of disguise to conceal the shape of the car. Large lumps of glass-fibre were bolted on and it ended looking like a Chieftain tank – very square and boxy.

"Once the EPs were running, we again had to create some kind of camouflage for them. Russ Varney, Paul Hunt and I came up with a scheme. We took an XJS bodyshell and asked MGA to square off the back end with foam, almost making it into an XJS estate. A mould was taken off that to make the camouflage, which was essentially in three pieces – a big, boxy rear end with a hatch that lifted up so you could reach the boot, a section that went round the front of the car and over the wings, and then a piece that went on the bonnet to hide the curves. We decided we had to screw these sections to the steel bodywork.

"There were a couple of scary moments when the

front bonnet piece came off at speed, but otherwise the camouflage worked well. We received a very nice compliment in an article on spy photography written by someone from Ford. He said that the new Jaguar was wearing so much camouflage that it was difficult to tell whether it's animal, vegetable or mineral! Fergus Pollock sent this to me and we felt we had succeeded! Keeping the car secret, in fact, was one of our bigger dilemmas."

The team could not wait to try the first EP to be completed, as Kevin Riches reveals. "Around eight of us, including Bob Dover, did some high-speed runs at Millbrook. We left Whitley at 7.00 one evening and cruised down the motorway with a black X100 and two Mondeos. At Millbrook we fitted a new set of reference tyres and, as it was dark, removed the camouflage. Mike

By any standards, the camouflage constructed for MP19 did a magnificent job of destroying its beautiful lines.

Cross, our ride and handling driver, took the car out and warmed it up.

"Then we all went round the track at various speeds, slowly building up. I was one of the last to drive and circled the track at maximum speed – 155mph. And there we were crawling round inside the car trying to feel for vibrations – looking back now it seems rather a curious way to behave! It was a prototype vehicle that had never been up to those speeds before, but it was lovely and quiet up to about 130-140mph. We completed the exercise at 2.00am, but we were in work the next day."

There were 28 EPs, two of them non-runners used for side-impact testing. A good proportion of the cars were allocated for electrical testing. Others were used for Timmins cold climate testing, Phoenix hot climate testing, wiper and washer work, seal development, power unit work, hot room testing, brake development, front and rear crash testing, and seat development.

Helen Atkins joined Jaguar during the X100 programme as a graduate engineer and was seconded to Kevin Riches at Body-In-White and Trim Engineering. Her responsibilities included seat development.

"We used a carry-over X300 switch pack built into the seat. But having additional height restrictions with the X100, together with the fact that we were using an XJS floor, meant there were some packaging constraints on the switch pack. With the integral headrests it's also very difficult to get a good, comfortable seat design – the seats were so style-driven.

"The Phase 1 seats that we saw on the EPs were awful and every single person who tried the cars complained that they felt incredibly uncomfortable. We had test drivers moaning bitterly about the switch pack dig-

The camouflage concocted for the Evaluation Prototypes rivalled that of MP19 for sheer ugliness. The only body area untainted by glass-fibre adornment was the roof – these views are actually of a Convertible!

X100 seat is based on a modified XJS seat frame with a new upper pressing to achieve a rather sportier appearance. Seen here are a design similar to the production version (left) and a sporty alternative (right).

ging them in the leg because the cushion was very thin.

"Solving this became a joke towards the end. We were up to Phase 18 before we came anywhere near an acceptable level of comfort, but by Phase 22 we'd cracked the problem and were just attending to minor tweaks and stitch patterns. I believe wholeheartedly that the style explains all the comfort difficulties we had.

"From a female perspective, I think women usually have different views on what we want from cars – and X100 is partly targeted at female customers. But everyone on the project recognised that it was important to make the car attractive to women buyers, particularly from an ergonomics point of view. Problem areas were examined on the EPs and we put an awful lot of women in those cars. Footwell concerns, for example, included high heels, small feet and extreme seat positions. Personally, I had a problem when driving because my knees made contact with the lower cowl on the column, and as a result we've made a bit more room there."

Noise, Vibration and Harshness (NVH) work really started with a vengeance on the EPs, so that the overall vehicle issues could be understood. Some work also had to be done to reduce under-bonnet temperatures. Thermal surveys were thought to have identified the issues, but a number of design changes led to some of the under-bonnet temperatures being higher than anticipated when the first EP was put into the hot room to measure them. The main cause turned out to lie in the fact that the manifolds and catalysts are close-coupled to improve emissions performance – catalysts are normally positioned under the floor. Ducting and heatshielding was then employed to reduce the hot spots.

"We've tested the temperature extremes, right up to 52 degrees C with full solar loading," states Chris Leadbeater, who by now had changed roles and succeeded Frank Marsden as Manager of the Sports Car Vehicle Office. "And we've protected for the extremes. This work was mostly done in the hot room, between February and December 1995. We have an emissions cell at Whitley that can reach 40 degrees C, so we did much of the initial development work here, looking at alternatives. To study the final sign-off effect, however, we went to Gaydon, where full solar loading is achieved with lamps simulating the midday sun.

"We picked the very worst case with the highest ambient temperature and highest solar loading, and then ran a series of city traffic type tests – stop/start, 20mph, idling, going up a gradient. We proved that the car can live under these absolutely worst-case conditions.

"Bob Dover, my Chief Engineer Paul Walker and I went to Timmins during the winter to understand how the EPs there were performing in cold weather testing. One of the test drivers wanted to demonstrate to us that he didn't think our winter tyres were that good on snow. It hadn't snowed for a few days, so he took us to a small country park where a bit more snow was lying. All seemed fine and his argument wasn't convincing, so he and Paul went down another road where the snow was deeper. There was a layer of ice and snow on top and, as they drove along, the car suddenly fell through the ice! We had some fun and games trying to dig it out."

One of Bob Dover's recollections serves to demonstrate the extreme conditions. When testing finished at 10pm, the team decided to dash the 300 yards from the

Much of the cold climate testing was carried out at Timmins, Canada, where the conditions could sometimes be a little too challenging. Even with traction control, a car cannot cope with really deep snow...

hotel to a hamburger joint. In spite of a full set of ski clothes, they only just made it. With the wind chill factor, the temperature was minus 50 degrees C...

After Timmins winter testing, EP33 went to Phoenix for summer testing and completed this in December. By the time this extended exercise finished, the car had covered 17,500 miles in a cold climate and 50,000 in a hot one. Another exercise during the summer was a high-speed durability test at Nardo, where EP20 ran faultlessly for 25,000 miles at close to maximum speed.

Other engineers had sessions at Timmins and Phoenix doing their own specific cold and hot climate testing. For example, fuel system engineers verified cold and hot fuel handling, and engine management people ensured that their calibrations worked throughout the temperature range. Transmission engineers, together with their colleagues from ZF, carried out a full assessment of their calibrations with their development aids, plugging their laptop computers, for instance, into the transmission to understand what was happening in detail.

Another company with whom Jaguar worked closely during this period was Teves, the brake suppliers. The braking system is effectively a carry-over from X300, on which a fairly significant change was made in 1994 by

moving from the Teves Mark 2 hydraulic system to the latest Teves vacuum booster system.

"In some respects changing to vacuum boosters might be considered a retrograde step because we used these years ago," states Ken Heap. "But while the hydraulic system has many advantages, there are some disadvantages too. These include pedal feel and sensitivity during gentle braking in traffic or just when holding the car in traffic jams. The old power booster needed a fairly high pedal effort in those situations.

"So the brake components carry over from X300 in virtually every respect, with the exception of the front

To measure the effect of the camouflage on performance, the EPs were tested 'fully clothed' in the MIRA wind tunnel.

discs. On the X100 we have taken advantage of the larger diameter base wheel specification to allow us to fit bigger ventilated front discs.

"ABS braking is constantly improving, and the important advance with X100 is that we've been able to offer a very sophisticated traction control system. To have a really good traction control system, you need a 'full authority' electronic throttle system from the engine. With this, the level of wheel slip generated at any time can be controlled far more accurately."

The ABS computer analyses the amount of slip at the driven wheels and tells the engine the precise level of torque it wants to match the amount of grip that it has calculated to be available. The engine responds to that command for torque and can make its own decisions: it will ultimately always close the throttle but this alone is not always fast enough, so it also has the options of reducing the fuel supply or switching off the ignition and literally shutting down cylinders to achieve very rapid torque reduction.

With camouflage removed, the makeshift rear lamps can be seen. Taken from a truck, they were a distinguishing mark of the EPs.

"Let me explain what would happen it you're driving on ice," continues Heap, "and you plant the accelerator pedal to the floor. The engine revs fly straight up, so to bring them back down very quickly the engine will cut its cylinders, cut its fuel and shut the throttle, and then with the shut throttle it will re-introduce the cylinders and the fuelling.

"A great deal of work was done over the winters of 1994 and '95 to optimise performance and feel in these conditions. We worked with our supplier to develop a slip strategy that allows the best take-off performance on any poor surface, whether it be snow, ice or wet roads. These conditions demand quite a lot of take-off slip, but it's necessary then to reduce that amount of slip as the car goes faster, in order to restrain the car's tendency, say, to oversteer in a corner if you're injudicious with the accelerator pedal.

"The brakes are involved in traction control, as with

any modern high-spec system – but we have two systems on the X100. We have the engine-based traction control system, loosely called Stability Control. Then we have the true Traction Control System, which includes the engine intervention feature but also has the ability to apply the rear brakes independently so that they operate like a limited slip differential. That's useful in split co-efficient conditions – where one wheel is on a high co-efficient surface and the other on a low co-efficient surface.

"The wheel on the low co-efficient surface will always tend to spin, and with an open differential it will actually spin to such an extent that you don't make much progress. So you can apply one rear brake to that wheel and allow the good wheel to drive the car away. That works extremely well in conditions typical of Sweden, where the roads are quite high-crowned for good drainage – ice forms in the gutters but the crown of the road remains dry.

"The car we benchmarked as being the best was the BMW 840, but we think we've achieved better hill-climbing performance and better system refinement, in terms of noise generated during operation. The BMW system evokes the ABS pump and modulator, so you hear pumps and valves working, whereas ours is significantly more refined. Our off-the-line acceleration in snow and ice is also better."

These suspension and braking systems were designed by Ken Heap and his engineers, then passed on to their colleagues in Ride, Handling and Refinement, a department then headed by Tony Cartwright. "Ken designed most of the hardware and basically I tuned it," is how Cartwright sums up their roles.

"I think the reason a Jaguar feels like a Jaguar is because it's developed on British roads," says Cartwright. "Our roads are distinctly different. Because many of our suppliers are German, we have tried in the past to do ride development in Germany, but it doesn't work because the roads there are very smooth and the auto-bahns are flat. The roads here – definitely those around Coventry – are ideal for working towards our traditional solutions, so we do most of this work nearby.

"Obviously we can't go very fast on public roads, so the proving ground at MIRA – not far away at Nuneaton – is a very important facility for us. The 'Dunlop Handling Circuit', which is very smooth with high grip and suited to aggressive handling, is used at speeds up to 80/90mph for cornering stability, to ensure that the car is safe and stable under all circumstances. It's essential that the car mustn't get the driver into trouble through a corner, no matter what he does – lift off the throttle, hit the brakes, do something daft, panic in some way. We want it to have high grip and go fast round corners, but above all it has to be completely safe, with benign on-the-limit handling.

Ride and handling work was largely carried out at the MIRA facility, near Nuneaton. Because convertibles are inevitably less stiff structurally than closed cars, the suspension has to be tuned differently to suit each model.

"There's also an old ride and handling circuit at MIRA, but frankly it's awful for tuning the handling because it's so bumpy. Deliberately it has lots of potholes, strange rippled surfaces, adverse cambers, railway crossings and dips, so we use it more for refinement work. It represents New York rather well!

"Mike Dale's particular favourite stretch of road is the journey from our US headquarters at Mahwah down to JFK airport, past the Bronx and over all the bridges. The surface is absolutely dreadful, with lots of deep potholes. He wants Jaguars to be best-in-class down there because he thinks plenty of our US customers drive along there. So we've been there, done that!"

Another challenging piece of road that has special significance is Southfield Freeway in Detroit. The main road on which Ford World Headquarters is situated, it has truck grooves that can make a car pull violently sideways, even though they are barely visible. For obvious reasons it is rather important that any Jaguar copes well with this little challenge, so a run along Southfield Freeway was included as a sign-off test...

"Another test track we use is the Pirelli facility at Vizzola," continues Cartwright. "I think the reason we go there is the food! Actually it's a good test track, tucked up in the hillside just outside Milan. It's quite small, but excellent for wet grip and there are aquaplane facilities – so we've been there once or twice a year to validate the wet grip. But while we can do a good deal of useful work on test tracks, there's no substitute for getting out on real roads in the wet and going past real trucks and under real bridges."

Mike Cross is a chassis system development engineer who works for Cartwright. He did most of the test driving and made decisions on the tune of tyres, damper settings, roll rates, steering progression and suchlike. At

Vizzola he set a new lap record for a production car – the previous best was by a Ferrari 456GT!

"We had an interesting trip to Germany during the summer of 1995," recalls Cross. "We drove out from here and did some uncamouflaged testing on the autobahn at night, looking at high-speed stability, wind noise, and the performance of headlights and wipers. We found ourselves a garage under a hotel in a very secluded part of Germany near the Nürburgring and based ourselves in

Pirelli's impressive wet-grip test facility at Vizzola, near Milan, was used every six months or so.

there, and ventured out once it was dark onto the autobahn to test the car at maximum speed.

"It was quite exciting because security was clearly important. We had a BMW 850 along for comparison, plus an Aston Martin DB7, an XJR and an XJS. We were extremely pleased with the stability of the X100. We also invited representatives from Jaguar Germany, who are notoriously difficult to please – but they said it was the best Jaguar ever."

On 13 June the Project Team discussed pulling forward Job 1, the completion of the first saleable car, from 5 August to 4 June, which would result in more cars being available for sale at launch. This was remarkable considering the tight time scale of the programme, but two days later the Board approved the change.

In mid-1995 rather indistinct 'spy' photographs appeared in *Autocar* and *Car*. They had been taken at Nardo during a brief period when EP20 ran with reduced camouflage because it was doing high-speed cooling tests, which clearly require representative airflow around the car. Silver foil and paint were applied to the headlamps to disguise them, but otherwise the distinctive front of the car was unadorned. Unfortunately the eight-mile Nardo test bowl can be overlooked from afar by long lenses...

"We feel that the balance between ride and handling is something of a Jaguar speciality," continues Cartwright. "Many of our competitor cars are excellent on handling and some are very refined, but it's rare for them to put the two together. We like to think we produce cars that are in the leadership area for refinement and comfort, yet have stunningly good handling too. With X100, we wanted to maintain the

A hard-top was considered for the Convertible and rejected, but may reappear in the future if there is sufficient demand.

The historic – and challenging – 14-mile Nürburgring circuit in Germany was another continental test venue.

Testing rigs, designed and built in-house, were used extensively during X100 development. Information was gathered from tests in the field and then recreated on rigs. This car is undergoing a simulated PASCAR test.

refinement side, but push forward in the areas of handling and confidence of driving, in line with the team's Mission Statement.

"Right at the beginning of the programme, we thought we would need to offer several ride and handling set-ups to cover the world markets. Traditionally the American market prefers a soft ride. The German market puts the priority on being able to travel very quickly with high levels of stability. The UK market is somewhere in between. We thought we'd probably need

four set-ups and named them Touring, GT, Sport and SuperSport. As we got into the development and lots more people – from Sales & Marketing, for example – started driving the prototypes, they realised the car was very fast and their image of it started drifting more towards 'sports' than it had been. So ultimately we cut out two of those derivatives."

Steering is an important factor in good ride and refinement, and Jaguar power steering has often been criticised for lack of feel and excessive lightness. As described in the previous chapter, variable assistance has been carried forward for X100 and variable ratio has been developed specially for it, but there is an additional feature.

Cycles of 100,000 door slams were carried out with this apparatus: assuming 10 door slams daily in real life, this equates to 27 years' use...

"The steering has a feature that ZF calls 'Positive Centre Feel' (PCF)," explains Cartwright. "It's a little trick mechanism they build into the power steering valve which effectively locks out the hydraulic part, just on centre, so that it gives you unassisted steering just for the first couple of pounds of effort. At high speed this gives a nice tight feeling for straight-line driving."

The only other comparable system, according to a proud Bob Dover, is the one fitted to the Ferrari

456GT. The cheaper Ferraris do not have this level of sophistication. Jaguar believes that, in ZF, it has worked with the best steering supplier in the world.

"We chose Pirelli tyres for the X100," continues Cartwright. "In the UK Pirelli are a relatively small operation, so they are able to respond to us well and technically they always come up with the best specification.

"In comparison with the XJS, we have gone for significantly wider tyres. This gave us a big task in terms of comfort, but a great advantage in terms of handling. The cleverness of the tyres is that they have an asymmetric tread. The outside is substantially the section that does the hard work when cornering, while the inside has drainage grooves to protect the aquaplaning position – so an asymmetric pattern gives a better balance between aquaplane performance and dry-road handling."

For the Sport option the largest possible tyres were chosen. They are known as 'Pirelli System', which means front and rear tyres are different sizes, and the fronts are 'handed'. To give the best compromise between steering, refinement and wet grip, it is better if the front tyres are designed to rotate in a specific direction. When the temporary spare is included as well, there are actually four different wheels and tyres on each car. "Doesn't suit Manufacturing – they hate it!" quips Cartwright.

"For the Sport option, we've increased the roll stiffness to make the car much more sporting, by stiffening the spring rates. We've also put electronic damping on the car, something we've wanted to do for a long time. We searched the world to find a system that worked for us, and finally came up with a solution from Bilstein that performs very well.

"Conventional dampers basically just contain a piston running in oil with some valve plates. This provides the ability to tune damping force relative to wheel velocity – you can play a lot of tunes on that and the subtleties of the valves and plates are very important. If you want to make the body really taut, to avoid the car floating up and down all the time like a saloon, you can achieve that with a conventional damper, but it always compromises the low-speed ride – so there tends to be a jerky ride with tight body control.

"An electronic system uses a small electrically-driven orifice inside each damper, controlled by an ECU that receives data from several accelerometers in the car. So, the car's driving along and it says, 'Hello! We're starting to exceed certain velocities, I need to tighten up the dampers'. This has given us wonderful freedom to tune the ride and handling, and we're extremely proud of the result."

Another department that comes under the umbrella of Chassis Engineering is Vehicle Refinement and Testing. Like Ken Heap, Tony Cartwright and Mike Cross, the staff here report to Paul Walker. In the past one group of people collected structural data from testing and another group ran the structural rig test laboratory. Walker decided it made sense to combine the roles.

"I felt that much more efficient synergy would come from them collecting their own data to run their own rigs. We've done a great deal of structural rig testing on this car, which has cut down the amount of complete vehicle testing – and speeded up some of it as well. And, of course, you obtain much better repeatability with a rig-controlled test than with a car out in the field."

Repeated door slams are just one example of the use of testing rigs. On the Verification Prototypes (VPs) that began build in September, cycles of 100,000 door slams were the norm. If any part failed, it was reported, monitored and improved for the next build phase.

Clever hydraulic engine mounts, supplied by Avon, make a notable contribution to refinement. Ordinary engine mounts consist of a slab of rubber between two plates. These have some inherent damping effect but offer little scope for tuning. A hydraulic engine mount, however, is filled with oil and acts like a car suspension damper. By careful design of the damping plates, cavities and stiffnesses, another dimension can be brought to tuning the engine mounts. Relative softness, and thus good isolation, can be created at higher frequencies, but much more stiffness is offered at lower frequencies.

"All through the programme," states Bob Dover, "we have been working to get good value and the maximum amount of feature. One of the ways we can do that most successfully is by using the 'parts bin' approach. So in X100 you may well recognise the air conditioning panel, door mirrors and upper steering column from the saloon. The 'J' gate gear selector is essentially a development of that used in the saloon. This approach does three things for us: it reduces development time, development cost and the number of parts that the business has to manage.

"The console lid is actually an X300 part in a different colour. Some of the switches will be seen in forthcoming Jaguar models. Where there's an advantage and it doesn't

In September 1995 the first examples of the 33 Verification Prototypes were completed. This Convertible, VP19, together with Coupé VP9, first endured the hardship of winter at Timmins and then experienced the other extreme in Arizona and Texas.

show, we've used a few Ford parts, including the security and door modules. In every area of the car we've looked around to find parts that are acceptable."

Dover is particularly pleased with the way suppliers have risen to the challenges, many and varied. "Arvin Cheswick supply the complete exhaust system – downpipe, catalyst and silencer. We wanted the engine to sound pleasing, so we did some benchmarking, using Ricardo Engineering, and tape-recorded numerous V8s in different cars. We then played those to a panel of people and decided between us which of the exhaust sounds we liked. Giving the tape to Arvin Cheswick, we asked them to match the favoured sound on top of their other obligations to meet back-pressure limitations, cost targets, timing targets, the supply of prototypes and the number of prototypes. They were very good and very responsive.

"Coventry Presswork make the complete fuel tank assembly for us and they are very strong on employee involvement. Whenever we were at a key stage, and fitting the fuel tank into the first buck was one of them, we had about 20 of their people around the buck. I couldn't get near it, which was just tremendous – wonderful enthusiasm."

The 33 Verification Prototypes (VPs) were constructed in late 1995 and early 1996. They had fully-tooled bodies with a large proportion of parts from production tooling. The purpose of these cars was to verify that all changes made to their predecessors, the EPs, were correct – they were to be the final engineering sign-off. But there was one slight hitch, as Kevin Riches recalls.

"The bonnets for the VPs, like all the VP panels, were actually pressed at Ogihara, so we sent our guys over to Japan specifically to see the bonnets go together. We sent across the adhesives, and the inners were clinched to the outers over there. The bonnets duly came back, but they were all incredibly weak. We couldn't understand it. We'd used all this super Knowledge Based Engineering. Poor Mark White was tearing his hair out.

"Finally we established that we'd given them the wrong adhesive – anti-flutter rather than structural! All the bonnets were completely scrap, but by then the tooling was on its way to the UK so we couldn't even get any more made. It was incredibly frustrating. We had to use the floppy bonnets, but in the end this wasn't a major problem because the camouflage bolted to them, ironically, added the necessary strength."

Two VPs, 9 and 19, went to Timmins for three weeks and then on to Toronto. They then each did 50,000 miles of humidity testing in Phoenix and went on to spend several weeks in Mexico for high-altitude and low-grade fuel testing. Cars were also tested in Denver, Colorado, at Pikes Peak for altitude, Death Valley in California, Corpus Christi in Texas, and in Florida.

"The original plan at Timmins was to run the cars for 25,000 miles, but we reduced the target to 17,500 to give them breaks to cool right down," states Russ Varney. "You can run them all round the clock and reach the mileage, but you never actually assess their performance when cold. Specifically for X100, we also built an outdoor fenced-off area so that we could leave the cars parked overnight without camouflage, just to be sure that they cooled right down.

"Throughout the process, one of the things we do in our area is assess the vehicles to understand if we are achieving our objectives. We have something called the VAG Process – Vehicle Assessment Group. It's a collection of people from different areas of the company who go through a detailed assessment form to understand what the vehicle's like. Each person drives the car over a route and assesses it based on those parameters. We measure these and report at the next Gateway."

An example from a VAG form includes many details of wash/wipe performance: swept area, effectiveness, intermittent delay, spray delivery when driving, and wiper obscuration when working and parked. When a VAG test is carried out on a vehicle, it is also done back-to-back with a competitor. This constant measurement of the standards achieved by the opposition removes any danger of Jaguar people losing sight of the way other manufacturers make progress too.

Two VPs covered 17,500 miles each in Timmins, then a further 50,000 miles each in Arizona and Texas. The purpose of the VPs, built largely from production tooling, was to verify all the changes that had been made at the EP stage.

"Very early on we started holding Performance Feel meetings," continues Varney. "A multi-disciplined group got together to look at all aspects of 'performance feel' and we benchmarked competitors. We tried to understand the factors that make a car feel good. It obviously goes deeper than areas like engine performance – right into details like throttle pedal loads, what the rev counter does and suchlike. We wanted the driving experience to be exceptional."

"I think Jaguar is fairly unique," claims Mike Cross, "in that we sell one chassis specification world-wide. The two most extreme markets are Germany, a very high-speed market with good roads, and the US, a lower-speed market with poorer roads. In Germany people drive very quickly and want a car to feel tight and sporty. The opposite is true in America, where the cars are often quite soft in character.

"Jackie Stewart has assessed X100 several times for us. Back in April 1995 we ran three cars with three differ-ent suspension configurations. The conclusions were that the car should be more sporty, and pretty much through-out the project we've made it more sporty – and people have liked it more as we've gone along.

"I've very much enjoyed doing the Sport suspension. This uses 18in wheels – 8in wide at the front, 9in at the rear – and I'm very pleased with how it's come out. It's very comfortable and very sporty – a true Jaguar."

Apart from being a former World Champion and one of the greatest racing drivers of all time, Jackie Stewart is respected for his views on production cars. His personal links with Jaguar go back a long way (his father owned a Jaguar dealership and Jackie even went on honeymoon in his early E-type), and today he has professional links as well via his work for Ford.

LAUNCH AND BEYOND – 1996

The next level of prototype cars to be manufactured, following the VPs, were the Functional Build cars. Their purpose was to check final details, such as noise, vibration and harshness (NVH).

At the dawn of another year, the countdown began in earnest with launch just nine months away. As that day of reckoning approached, the tension was mounting. Public launch, if all went according to plan, would be 2 October.

The launch plan was split into three phases. The first phase, scheduled for February, was Functional Build (FB), for which 30 cars were built to undertake various tasks, including engineering final sign-off, homologation, advertising, press, photographic and show work. The intention was for them to be manufactured almost entirely off production tools, to include all options, and to represent all market territories – so this might be called a first dress rehearsal. The next phase, due to start in April and called 4P, comprised 111 basically saleable cars, 30 of which were earmarked towards an intended batch of 50 cars for Management Evaluation. These would be driven as if they were customer cars, so that they could be assessed in everyday use. Volume Build would – and did – start with Job 1, the first true production car, on 4 June and was planned to rise quite quickly to the normal production rate. From the first 170 cars built, 20 would be taken to complete the Management Evaluation batch of 50.

"We are into the very last changes and tuning now," commented Dover in the spring. "For all final phases of build, apart from the first EPs, every car has been built down the final assembly track. That has been an

extremely valuable training aid, and has also allowed us to use the production water testing facility, the production noise testing rigs, and so on."

It is relatively unusual to have Field Evaluation Units – those cars in the batch of 50 – in the public domain before launch, but this is another example of the search for perfection. The intention has been to put finished XK8s through as much real-world usage as possible, in order to check how they perform before customers start receiving them.

"I've just come back from Timmins," stated Chris Leadbeater in March, "where the VPs are running. The test drivers, without prompting, were all very impressed with the progress we'd made. We had some of our most vocal criticisms of the seats with the EPs, but they're satisfied now. These people virtually live in the cars. They go out on shift eight hours a day and drive, have a break, and drive again. Their opinions really do count."

With the cars still camouflaged, the spy photographers were ever active. Early in the year, Mike Cross was followed from Whitley to Browns Lane. He stopped at a pedestrian crossing and someone pulled his car alongside, jumped out and started taking shots through the window. Fortunately the police were two cars back and they discussed with him the fact that he had abandoned his car in the middle of the road!

Paul Stokes gives an overview of how the programme developed through its final stages. "We have a

Chief Programme Engineer, who was involved with X100 from the start, and as the programme came closer to the main assembly tracks we brought in a Chief Launch Engineer, Colin Tivey. Initially you might think that it would make sense to have the same person doing both roles, but it's necessary for somebody to work in the plant alongside David Hudson – Director, Production Operations – bringing the car through, sucking it through Engineering, and also being very critical of the vehicle that has to be built. He must be able to go to Engineering and say that he doesn't like any detail of fit or finish. This kind of system worked very well on the X300 programme."

Bob Dover takes up the thread. "Everything from the production release on the X300 saloon programme was handled by a Launch Team, which was another of Jim Padilla's innovations based on North American experience. This was run by Colin Tivey. One of the lessons learned from X300 was that the team should start earlier, and should be more integrated. For X100, therefore, we put a lot of the Project Team people on to the Launch Team to make sure there's a seamless continuity of people, skills, knowledge and process, and that they know and understand the suppliers."

Colin Tivey's responsibility has been to ensure that the XK8 is launched at the pre-determined quality levels, within the programme budget, and on time. His Launch Team was formed during 1995, but the action and intensity stepped up as launch approached. The team consisted of 80 to 100 people located at the Browns Lane assembly plant, and included product engineering, process, purchasing and planning people – indeed they covered all facets of the company.

"A typical day would begin at 7.30am with a Start-Up Meeting," explains Tivey. "This was a funnel for all issues, wherever they'd been raised, whether it be Timmins, or Phoenix, from Whitley, from Build, from the quality review, or a vehicle drive assessment. So representatives from the whole of the team would be there – probably 30 people. We would start off by raising all the concerns, which would be documented and loaded on to the computer. Typically 50 to 60 issues would take us up to about 7.45am. At that point we would communicate what would be happening that day so that everyone had a common base of knowledge about exactly where we were. By the very nature of what we do, it's fast-moving and extremely dynamic – so good communication is absolutely essential.

"From 8.00am through until just before 11.00am, we would hold a series of short Exceptions Meetings. Each of the areas – we'd start with the body people, then move through trim, electrical, chassis, power train, process, purchasing, vehicle office – would come in as a group with their outstanding problems, which would already have gone through a Start-Up Meeting some days earlier. They would explain the exceptions that weren't meeting the timing criteria.

"Early on, when we had just started the build, we had a criterion that demanded 50% of all problems should be solved within five days. Once we moved into the FB phase, we shortened that time to two days. So if a problem had been raised two days earlier and hadn't been addressed, the person responsible would have to explain why. These meetings would be very short, very sharp and very focused, driving the individuals concerned because they knew they had to attend and report back daily.

"Then at 11.00am we would have a Release Meeting. It's almost a cycle. Some time earlier things will have gone through the Start-Up Meeting. Then, if it hasn't been fixed, it will have gone through the Exceptions Meetings. And then eventually it will come to the Release Meeting, where all the documentation is available to enable Purchasing to go away and buy the part, or for

Process to make the change. That leaves the rest of the day to force issues through and to make sure that exceptions are driven out.

"Our concerns can be defined as quality, cost and timing, but actually the focus of the team is almost 100% on quality. If there's a quality issue that costs money, we'll find the money to fix it – no question. So we make no excuses for focusing totally on quality, very much to the detriment of timing in many instances – if we don't have the parts and they're not to the correct standard, we won't build the car.

"As we start to build cars ahead of Job 1, our focus is very much on our internal indicators for quality. Once a prototype is completed, the first thing that happens to it is a visit to an area called the Customer Focus Centre. Here it's visually inspected in detail, looking for poor fits and gaps, for missing components, for scratches, dings and dents. There's a scoring process, and the higher the score the worse the car.

"If the staff there give a problem a 'nine', it indicates that 90% of customers, in their opinion, would notice it.

'Job 1', the first customer XK8, was completed on 4 June. Bob Dover, who led the XK8 Project Team, was there to see it come off the line, complete with protective padding around its nose.

So obviously the team's intent is to drive that score down to zero. We develop 'road maps' that take us from where we are with particular scores towards that zero. That process takes probably two to three hours, and then we sit down with the score, as a team, and establish 'ownership' for those issues – and then they will be raised at the 7.30am Start-Up Meeting. So this process amounts to a vital quality indicator. Another quality indicator is Build Concerns, and these are brought up at the same meeting.

"We also have a process called NovaC – New Overall Vehicle Assessment, plus a 'C' for Customer. This shares the scoring system used by the Customer Focus Centre, but the car is taken on a 40-mile drive. The static and dynamic marks are combined, and again a score is given. And then we go through the same problem-solving process – a review around the car, 'ownership' of the issues, driving the issues back through the system.

"Sitting on top of this micro management, which solves all the problems that occur, is the macro version. Each month we have a Launch Review that's normally chaired by the Vehicle Line Director, Jim Padilla."

To obtain a first-hand impression of these important Launch Reviews, I sat in on one. They are attended by Bob Dover, Clive Ennos, Mike Beasley, David Hudson, all the Chief Engineers and the launch engineers. Others come and go as required. It is a fairly tense, terse and

Until relatively late in the day, the car was to have dark grey rear bumpers. But fashions change and it was decided that colour-keyed bumpers would be preferred by customers in 1996 and beyond. Note the non-production badges, including one describing the car as an XJS!

structured meeting which lasts six to eight hours. It begins with Colin Tivey giving an introduction to bring everybody up to date. There is a NovaC overview, then the meeting moves through a series of engineering issues and testing status reports. The engine programme is discussed, but the bulk of the meeting, probably two to three hours, is taken up talking through Open Concerns.

At one stage there were 4700 Open Concerns, but by this meeting, on 8 March, this had been reduced to 140. Some 64% of Open Concerns were being closed within two days, and from the following Monday that would be raised to 70%.

Jim Padilla sat in the centre of a U-shaped table with around 50 people in the room at any one time. Every so often he would fire off a searching question, throw in a telling observation, request more urgency, or contribute a constructive suggestion. He does not shirk from giving a colleague a hard time if he deserves it. You can feel the pressure everyone is under, but equally the atmosphere is very positive. Padilla calls it "sweating the details".

"There are no alibis," he says. "Sometimes you have to say to a guy, 'You made a commitment. I'm not the judge, the customer's the judge. You've promised something, don't fall short'. In a way it's not what happens in the meeting that counts – it's what happens in the preparation for the meeting."

The original Project Team had a board in the Project Control Room, or the 'War Room' as it was called, that displayed a countdown in days to Job 1. The Launch Team inherited the idea, which similarly focused minds and instilled a sense of urgency.

"The atmosphere within the Launch Team tends to build almost to a crescendo," states Tivey. "At the 7.30am Start-Up Meeting we have people almost clamouring to take problems away as their own. Almost without exception, you have to say, 'Look, hang on a minute. Are you sure that's your problem?' That in itself is a testament to the enthusiasm of the people on the team. There really is a tremendous, electric atmosphere as we get towards the launch."

Jeff Key was one of three Launch Managers working for Colin Tivey. "The VP build stage generated over 2000 Concerns. So the scale is perhaps difficult to comprehend. One would think that once Engineering had released a design, that was it – but that clearly isn't the case. We have, perhaps, 2000 components on the car that change after release. There's a standing joke within the Launch Team that every component changes three times, but statistically that's exactly what happens up to launch – it's incredible. And we're not unique. That's generic within the motor industry. They are minor in terms of the change, but pretty major in terms of the effect on the vehicle."

Another key member of the original team from the early days was Tony Duckhouse, whose responsibility is Finance. "When the car was handed over to Colin Tivey's team, in theory Engineering had released it and all their design work was complete, but it doesn't actually work like that. From then on it should be the case that the only people who change the design of the car, and therefore its investment or piece cost, are the team we call the Pink List. Every time any change is proposed to the car, it has to go to the Pink List to decide whether it's accept-

able or not. They assess it in terms of cost, investment, timing and quality.

"You have to recognise that Sales & Marketing take a view at the beginning of a programme of what they want and then as time goes on they change their minds. That's not because they're fickle. It's because the market has changed and what was acceptable at a Styling Review in 1993 is not acceptable in 1996.

"'There's a good example. The original car had grey bumpers. That went though all the Styling Reviews and the dealers saw it. Everyone said, 'Great'. Now the car has colour-keyed bumpers and that's acceptable as well, but it was a change and it cost us money. I have to recognise that the market now appeared to demand colour-keyed bumpers and try to accommodate that within my total variable-cost figure.

"A colour-keyed bumper sounds easy, but there are 12 colours and you have to segregate them. You have to tell your suppliers what colours you want, and that's much more expensive that saying, 'Send me a load of grey ones'."

One of the durability tests that was being employed in the latter half of 1995 and continued during 1996 is known as PASCAR. It is a new Ford test programme. Ford decided that it wanted to try to understand more closely how a customer uses his or her car. Black boxes were installed in various cars to record the structural inputs during the typical lifetime of cars around the world. All those test results were then combined and split down into block programmes of the different surfaces that a car would encounter over its entire life.

PASCAR 1, which takes about six weeks, is a relatively low-mileage test but there is a high structural input.

PASCAR 2, which takes 160 days, simulates normal usage but is accelerated: the cars do 43,560 miles with 133 cycles of 332 miles each, which translates to 100,000 miles of 'real' use.

There is no better way of understanding something than experiencing it first-hand. As a consequence Russ Varney organised for me to spend at afternoon at MIRA while the PASCAR tests were still in progress. Abe Bhayat drove me there in Convertible VP20 and Nick Gilkes took me round, first in Coupé VP51.

We began by lapping the Ride and Handling circuit at 40mph. Built into this metalled road surface are the sort of features you would expect to find on any public road in North America or Europe. They include a section that makes the car pitch, followed by adverse cambers, steep cambers, railway crossings and potholes. A complete PASCAR 1 test would consist of 1024 laps of the Ride and Handling circuit.

The next section I experienced is known as the Cow Pats or River Bed Crossing. Raised discs of concrete, roughly the size of cow pats, sit 2-3in high and are crossed at about 2mph. These put loads into the suspension corners that twist the body and the suspension mounting points.

The Corrugations came next. These are 0.375in high and spaced at 5in intervals. Taken at 30mph, they excite the suspension and are good for imposing loads on suspension and body fixings. They certainly generate considerable vibration through the car.

Then on to the Chuck Holes, which replicate the potholes typical of North American cities. The first set is taken at 16mph, the second set at 34mph. These potholes, which are 100mm (3.9in) deep, are square-edged

During 1995 and '96 X100 prototypes tackled a series of durability tests grouped together under the title of PASCAR 1. These vicious lumps of concrete are known as the Cow Pats or River Bed Crossing.

and not too friendly – in fact positively brutal. Pothole strikes put 40g on the stub axles – a colossal load – and about 10g through the bodyshell.

"Those were the Ladders," stated Gilkes as we pressed on, "in phase and out of phase at 12mph." The speed is critical because of the amount of resonance that is set up in the body. Had we driven over the rungs at

The Chuck Holes simulate surfaces more prevalent in North American cities than European ones. These brutal, square-edged potholes are 4in deep and are taken first at 16mph and then at 34mph.

Traversing the Ladders provides data about suspension and body resonances, allowing vibration periods to be eliminated.

Crossing this 6in high kerb at 50mph is another way of torturing the suspension.

30mph, the effect would have been barely noticeable. But at 12mph the height of the rungs and the distance between them puts maximum loading into the suspension and structure.

The Stone Road, which simulates typical rural tracks in North America, is traversed at 30mph. Over 1000 passes are made during the test, giving useful information

about the effect of stone pecking on body-in-white areas, sill panels, underfloor components, brake pipes, fuel pipes, locating clips and bushes. Apart from physical damage to the structure and other components, the test confirms whether the car is sealed properly against dust and grit. Another test activity involves coating the car with fine dust to check that no problems occur.

The Postel Road simulates roads in Europe where cobble stones have been covered in tarmac or areas of tarmac have eroded. During ABS braking stops on this surface, the different coefficients of friction – caused by the cobbles alternating with the tarmac – work the brakes extremely hard, and in turn the suspension is worked hard as well, particularly in the longitudinal direction.

Passing over the Long Wave Pitch at 30mph is a harsh test of front and rear suspension dampers, which are put through alternate periods of severe bump and rebound. This is an effective way to identify any damper problems quickly – the car should not show any tendency to crab over or pitch dramatically.

Kerb Island is another test aimed mainly at usage in North America, where kerbs tend to be higher than in Europe. I had been warned that this is an unbelievable test and it did not disappoint. Nick Gilkes just drove, at an oblique angle, at a 6in kerb at what seemed like an outrageous speed – 50mph – in the circumstances. The poor car took it in its stride. A total of 64 such passes throughout the whole test simulate what the most unimaginably brutal driver might do to a car in the course of its lifetime...

PASCAR 1 also includes sections of the traditional, car-breaking Belgian pavé, work on test hills, figures of eight, and turning the steering lock to lock while stationary. The total effect amounts to a breath-taking degree of car vandalism!

For a sample of PASCAR 2, Nick Gilkes and I jumped into Convertible VP11, which had already undergone the rigours of PASCAR 1. Again the plan of attack for the test is mapped out strictly.

Initially the car does four laps of the Ride and Handling circuit at 50mph, with accelerations to 80mph. Then it goes on to do a Transient Test – 70mph to 90mph. Next comes a high-speed cycle, which comprises

36 laps of the banked circuit at MIRA. Speed is increased progressively to the maximum, which means a restriction of 110mph on the banking and whatever the car will manage down the straight.

"We are running on the banking at 110mph," commentates Gilkes, "and now taking it up to a genuine 120mph on the straight. Round the banking again, now kicking down as we come out of the bend, full throttle back to 120mph, cruising the rest of the straight at 120, bend coming, overrun down to 110, and we're into the bend again. These bends are quite severe and tyre wear is a consideration. We are running at 42psi with dedicated tyres for high-speed testing."

Other attempts to damage the long-suffering durability cars include passing through a mud bath of 25mm depth at 12mph. The whole car, top and bottom, is covered in a film of unsavoury filth. A salt trough of similar depth, taken at 35mph, attempts to corrode everything that the Stone Road has managed to chip or blemish. Acceleration tests on volcanic Basalt Tile, which has a low coefficient of friction, are considered good for testing both ABS stops and traction control acceleration.

Meanwhile, back at Browns Lane, the plant was gearing itself up, as David Hudson explains. "As we moved into the launch phase and the Project Team approach was handed over to Colin Tivey, I became very much part of the process. I started to take responsibility for actually building the prototypes, because we built them at Browns Lane in the Prototype Build area with my people.

"As more and more of the hourly-paid employees became involved, we trained the Group Leader and one other person from each zone in all the tasks that would be required of them. We verified their training, to ensure that they were competent, and they in turn became the trainers. While the Launch Team were talking product, the Manufacturing side were asking a load of questions of themselves. Are we managing the people? Are we training them? Do we have the right tools in place? Are the statistical tools in place? Do we understand what we are measuring? Have we set ourselves targets?

"We have had to extend the production line and put an engine marriage system in. With the XK8, we do the engine marriage in a totally different way. Instead of lowering the body onto the powertrain, we actually set the powertrain on a plinth, effectively a very accurate jig, and offer the plinth up to the body."

Trevor Crisp: "The whole manufacturing process is designed to ensure that when the engine, transmission,

Belgian pavé has been the main element in durability testing for several decades: 1000 miles on this car-breaking surface is said to equate to 100,000 miles of normal motoring.

The Mud Bath, taken at 12mph, soon reveals whether a car's seals are good enough. Even the roof becomes filthy, and photographer Mike Cann did not escape as he nobly stuck to his post!

Having been subjected to a generous peppering on other delights such as the Stone Road, the victim is then drenched in corrosive liquid as it is forced to dash through the Salt Trough at 35mph.

prop shaft and axle assembly go up into the car, everything is very accurately aligned."

XJS production ran at 110 units per week, whereas XK8 output is planned at 250 units – and only 115 people are building the cars. The new car is 30% quicker to build than its predecessor, an improvement achieved, in part, by buying in larger sub-assemblies. This has been made possible by the choice of best-in-class suppliers who can guarantee the integrity of their components and assemblies. It is a radical change from the late eighties, when Jaguar was manufacturing its own exhaust systems, radiators and door frames.

"The role for my team as launch approached," says Hudson, "was to ensure that we were achieving the objectives that had been set for the car. The onus was very much on the Manufacturing team in these latter stages. We had to work seven days a week. We work 12 hours a day as a norm anyway, but this spell meant doing even more. Achieving a world launch means getting the cars there, and you only do that by putting in the hours.

The way engines are installed in bodies has changed for XK8 production. The engine is now fixed to a plinth – effectively a very accurate jig – before 'marriage' takes place from below.

"Inevitably there are glitches, supply problems and engineering changes in the final stages. That's why we planned to have a 'batch and hold' facility. The intention was that I would build from 4 June and hold every car until well into August. So I always knew I'd have in the order of 2000 cars held here pending the final checks and tests.

"So if someone reports, 'At 40 degrees in Death Valley, when the car's parked at a certain angle at two minutes past two, this piece of trim discolours in the corner', we change it! The task is to ensure, above all, that we achieve our quality objectives – otherwise we don't ship cars."

"We have good new body-in-white facilities at Castle Bromwich," states Manufacturing Director Mike Beasley. "We had some technical difficulties when we first used them, but now we're achieving dimensional accuracy in body construction that we've never seen before – I'm very pleased indeed. This is a good example of the enthusiasm here. The production guys, the maintenance guys, the product engineers and the manufacturing engineers just threw themselves into a team and got stuck in. Inside a couple of months miracles were wrought. It's another example of great teamwork."

Having achieved Ford's Q1 status in 1993, the plants petitioned early in 1996 to be the first within Ford to be awarded the new Q1 Re-certification. David Hudson claims that, by the time of the XK8's launch, the Jaguar plants had become the best performers throughout the Ford world on preventative maintenance, having come from behind.

Manufacture of the new AJ-V8 power unit takes place in a dedicated area within the Ford engine plant at Bridgend in South Wales. One or two purist eyebrows may be raised at this but it makes eminent sense, as Jim Padilla explains.

"This brings some positive synergy because we can take advantage of the high-volume manufacturing expertise within Ford Motor Company, and the efficiencies that come with that, while using the high-tech engineering prowess of Jaguar. It's a perfect match.

"A real success story in all of this has been the tremendous team work between the engine designers and Jaguar's own process engineers, who began the manufacturing process, and then gradually handed that over to Ford. People at the Bridgend plant have been very responsive – everybody wants to work on the Jaguar line."

Purchasing Director Paul Stokes achieved a considerable accolade both for himself and Jaguar when, in November 1995, he was promoted to the same position within Ford, with responsibility for rear-wheel drive cars. In that capacity, he is responsible for more than $10 billion expenditure per annum.

"This job meant I kept my Jaguar responsibility, but

also gave me the opportunity to gain much more experience. I think that has helped in all sorts of odd ways with suppliers to Jaguar who are also major suppliers to Ford. I can see areas of synergy. I don't think it's going to change the product, but it's certainly going to have an impact on the bottom line.

"We have achieved efficiencies at Jaguar over the past four years that have outstripped most of the industry, but we've kept very quiet about them. There was a time when Jaguar would have made lots of noise about this. We've had various Chairmen and at one time the idea was always to trumpet this sort of achievement in the press, but more recently we've damped things down and got on quietly."

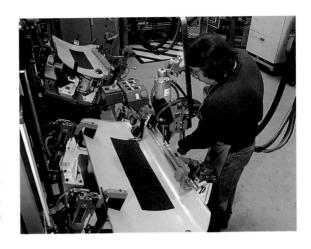

To cite one example of efficiency improvement, Stokes discovered how much Jaguar's Swedish transport company was charging Ford for transportation. Not surprisingly, Ford was paying rather less than Jaguar. He went to see the company and came away not only with a vastly better deal for Jaguar, which saved several million pounds, but also a better deal for Ford.

"In four years I've never yet had to threaten a supplier with Ford. But equally, people know I have a big brother and they don't really want a fight. They want to take a business decision if they can.

"I'm happy with the way the cost side of XK8 has gone. We've brought the car in under budget on variable cost. On capital costs we've just overspent on the body and just underspent on the engine. So overall we've balanced the books.

"I recently told the buyers to go back to the suppliers and ask them what the final tooling costs are. At the end of the exercise, you need to go back and close

the loop. There will be £10,000 left out of this one, £5000 left out of that one, and so on. Only yesterday I said, 'Go rake the leaves', because we might just get it absolutely on the button."

Bob Dover's heroic role was not yet over through the spring of 1996, although the end was in sight. With just a few months to go before launch, he was still motivating, chasing, persuading, organising and encouraging. He was still travelling the world in his search for the ideal answer to every challenge. Not quite everything went according to plan, though, as Paul Walker recalls with a smile.

XK8 bodies are assembled at Jaguar's Castle Bromwich factory, where Spitfire aircraft were built during the war. A door is spot-welded in its assembly jig; one in every 10 underframes is removed from the line for inspection in this jig; bonnet and boot lid have adhesive applied robotically before the outer panel is folded around the inner strengthening member; bodies move towards final assembly prior to fitting of the side panels in the main framing jig; key dimensional checks are made after framing, door apertures here being assessed for size and profile with the yellow master jigs.

"Bob Dover and I ended up in a ditch in Sweden with one of the VPs. Bob was very busy thinking about something else on this very snowy and cold road, and suddenly the piece of road he was driving on wasn't there any more – we were in soft snow. We ended up in the ditch and I was unable to get out of the car because I was in a snow bank on my side. Ken Heap has a bit of reputation for finding the handling limits of prototypes, and Bob's first remark on coming to rest was, 'This unfortunately means I'll have to be much more polite to Ken Heap in future!'"

Jim Padilla sums up Dover's role. "Bob is the integrator. Bob is the leader. Bob is accountable for the ultimate outcome. He has a lot of strong support in that regard. Bob has done an outstanding job of pulling together the programme and delivering it into the production environment, ready for the strong launch teams to drive the thing home. At this point, Bob's job has moved into

It is not easy to distinguish the road from the ditch in Lapland. Bob Dover failed to!

other areas – launching the car through the media and into the marketplace. That's a big function.

"You start with market input, from there you develop image targets for your vehicle, from there you develop metrics relative to the functional characteristics, and from there you develop the hardware assumptions. Then you execute the hardware assumptions, within the quality, cost and timing parameters, and drive to deliver. That was Bob's job."

The late David Boole, as Public Relations Director, had considerable influence on the decision concerning a name for X100. As a staunch supporter of Jaguar's heritage, he rightly insisted on XK.

"David was always the key driver on the naming policy, as he was for the XJ series," states Chairman Nick Scheele. "We also consulted Sales & Marketing, the Ad agencies and Mike Dale, who did some research in the US. David was then asked to pull all this guidance

The late David Boole insisted that the name of the new sports car should have the prefix XK, but there was debate as to what suffix might complete the job. Once the name was decided, it was necessary to choose a badge style. The winner, the bottom one, looks the right choice from this selection.

together and come up with a recommendation.

"The titles that came forward were XKF, XK8 and XK160. We decided against XKF largely because MG came out with the MGF. We thought that would be confusing, but the market research, interestingly enough, also indicated that XKF might be misunderstood as standing for Ford – and there's also an F Series truck in the US to add confusion.

"XK160 we thought was too retro. It would appeal to the buffs who knew what 120, 140 and 150 were, but it would mean little to the new audience we were trying to attract. So we went for XK8 and we're all very happy with it."

Bob Dover had been pressing his colleagues for a decision on the name, in part because the rear badge has a rather important hole in it – the emergency access to the boot through which a key is inserted.

"On one occasion," recalls Dover, "I was talking to Nick Scheele on his car 'phone and he happened to have David Boole and Roger Putnam with him. I said that while the three of them were together, why didn't they decide the name? There was then a long silence and I thought I must have said the wrong thing. As I couldn't wait any longer, I decided to chance it and released the XK8 badging. David called me later and said that they'd decided on XK8!"

Roger Putnam and his colleagues in Sales & Marketing had been involved with X100 from the start, of course, but now their role was about to come to the fore as the crucial launch approached.

"For the first time ever, to my knowledge, Jaguar has planned to pre-launch. I choose those words very carefully because prior to the nineties Jaguar pre-launched lots of cars without meaning to! But in those days the company didn't actually manage to build them once it had launched them...

"When you're only producing two models, it's very difficult to pre-launch a replacement for one of them because, inevitably, you kill the old model when you do so. In this case, due to the success of X300, we were able to run out the XJS very carefully. There was no danger of our dealers sitting on stocks of XJSs, as happened in the seventies when lots of E-types remained unsold for an awfully long time.

Like the E-type in 1961, the XK8 was unveiled at the Geneva Motor Show in 1996. But unlike the E-type, it was not a complete surprise, thanks to spy photography.

"So our plan was to show the car early and then gradually roll out the information: first sight of the car in March, details about the engine in June, specification and price during the summer. We did this in order to pre-sell as many cars as possible."

Just like the E-type, the XK8 was revealed to the public at the Geneva Show in March. The bonnet was locked down as the engine was still secret and, in fact, the under-bonnet style had yet to be finalised. Jim Padilla was among the senior Jaguar management there for the big moment.

"The Geneva Show was spectacular and the Jaguar stand was in an outstanding position. We had this huge, wooden crate with the Jaguar 'growler' motifs on it and the Jaguar 'leaper' coming out of the top. After the Chairman introduced some of the key members of the team, the crate lifted up to reveal the Coupé, which is just a beautiful piece of sculpture. And it was in a strikingly bright royal blue colour.

"Many of the people in the audience were stunned. The colour was so vibrant and it really did show off the flow of the body. We had people jammed around the stand all day – real encouraging. Several of the Jaguar executives gave interviews all day.

"We promised the media that the performance feel and the vehicle dynamics would match the promise of the exciting styling. We told them that, with the new V8 engine, we would have performance better than the V12 and fuel economy better than the straight-six.

"During the day someone said to me that he wished us luck. If you have good processes and good people, if you have good metrics, and if you are paying attention every day to the details, luck is not a factor. My management philosophy is that, if you can't measure it, you usually can't manage it. So when working with people, or working with teams, you start by saying, 'What are you going after? What are your objectives? What are your image targets? Who are you trying to beat in this game?'

"We benchmarked the best. You choose where you want to be different, what characterises your car. It's not good enough just being the same as everybody else. That's the Lexus mistake. Build in some personality – that's what Jaguars have – and don't ever lose it."

"At this point in time the patient was heading for the operating theatre," states Paul Stokes. "Everybody was getting anxious, which always happens at this stage in a programme. You could feel a little bit more tension in the air. There was a quickness in everybody's step. You had Jim flying in from America every two or three weeks, and I was coming back every five weeks."

As Job 1, the first true production car, went through bang on schedule – out of the Body Shop on 20 April, out of the Assembly Hall on 4 June – the planning was already in place to determine the mix of models that would be built to satisfy the various markets. The conclusion was that three Convertibles needed to be built to every two Coupés.

Some of the logistical complexities of a world-wide launch involved areas that most customers would never even think of. For example, during May attention had to be focused on the transportation of cars all over the world prior to launch. The availability of ships and where they would be docking had to be examined and bookings made, so that Jaguar could plan how many cars needed to be available, and at what time, to put them on the requisite ships to meet the launch date in every market. "It's no good me building a car for Europe if it's actually required for Japan," says David Hudson.

"The actual launch in the USA was set for 3 October," says Mike Dale, "but we did a number of things to start exciting the American public before that. One beautiful piece of timing occurred when the New York Museum of Modern Art decided to take an E-type into its collection and make it a permanent exhibit – quite an honour. We had the media moving in and out of a reception there on 3 April and the day culminated in a dinner for several hundred journalists – quite the biggest ever gathering of journalists around Jaguar in North America.

"At that dinner the head of the museum, myself and Geoff Lawson spoke, taking the E-type first of all and talking about keepers of history like the museum, like writers and like Jaguar itself. Geoff discussed the whole business of the styling of XK8. The exercise gave us an enormous amount of press and PR in North America, and that's far more valuable to us than advertising. The USA is so huge that if I spent $200 million advertising XK8, our share of voice wouldn't be that great. My advertising budget wasn't a tenth of that, so we had to use other weapons.

"The following morning, at 10.00, we unveiled the Convertible and the Coupé at the New York Show. This is exactly what Jaguar did with the E-type: the Coupé was launched in Geneva and the Convertible in New York. In one sense the parallel may seem a little corny, but it wasn't to us. That history is important to us. If we don't keep that sense of the importance of all these details, we shall lose what Jaguar is. That would be a great loss to the whole world."

"We have a very exciting advertising campaign," enthuses Roger Putnam. "It's based on all the work we did in the autumn of 1995 on brand strategy. We have understood the key elements of the brand strategy – the emotional appeal of the car, the heritage, the success of the E-type – and all the excitement that Jaguar generates. But we were also aware of the downside of the brand: all that Britishness is actually a two-edged sword.

"Britishness means different things in different markets. One strength is the quality evoked by things like Savile Row suits and Chippendale furniture, which bring connotations of craftsmanship, status and exclusivity. The downside is the perception of a cottage industry, low technology, bad quality perhaps, poor finish, poor design – a high level of conceptual engineering that tends to be let down by poor execution.

"So all these elements were drawn together to give

The XK8 was revealed at Geneva by lifting the crate under which it had been lurking. This was to have been accompanied by 'dry ice', but a dummy run with an XJS the day before covered the car in a greasy film...

The XK8's bonnet was firmly locked down and no details of specification or price were given. The Times even stated that the car had a Ford engine!

Again like the E-type, the XK8 Convertible was launched at the New York Show. Approximately 60% of all XK-E production went to the US, which is also the XK8's most important market.

us a brand strategy. It became obvious that nowadays, to compete on a level playing field, we must have a well-balanced mix of the emotional and the rational. And the rational can only be supported by competitive high technology, competitive quality, competitive reliability, competitive durability and competitive feature.

GRACEFUL.   ANIMAL.

The all-new 32 valve, AJ26 (Advanced Jaguar) engine powers
the new Jaguar XK8 to 156mph. And from 0-60 in just 6.5 seconds.
Graceful the Jaguar may be. But tame? Never.

JAGUAR XK8

THE

CAT

IS

BACK.

Stages in J. Walter Thompson's development of launch advertising: the 'Graceful/Animal' theme assessed early on; the communication strategy summary that introduced 'The Cat Is Back' slogan; and the finished ad.

"We then questioned what thought process best carries this balance forward. We thought of the animal itself, with the power of its shape and strength. The jaguar is an efficient creature that survives in some of the most difficult terrain in the world. Thus the animal itself would be a wonderful way to embody the Jaguar brand strategy.

"So the advertising with which we have launched XK8 is basically underwritten by the theme 'The Cat Is Back'. We hope this will evoke memories of the E-type and the animal itself. The adverts are not over-humorous, but thought-provoking and intended to bring a wry smile to the face. There are little puns to do with the animal. For example, the Convertible is being launched with the strap line, 'One Cat. No Hot Tin Roof'.

"There's a range of ads that we can choose from that link the car to the 'Cat Is Back' theme, and link also to a very powerful visual image of the car against a wild background with one headline and very little copy."

Special plans were made for North America – the most important market. The advertising would lead off on the night of 3 October all across the USA. At least five XK8s would be on show at every dealer, and there would be dealer parties all across the USA.

"If we sell to the walls by 31 December," says Mike Dale, "we shall have sold 2200 cars in the US in the first three months – our ambition is to do exactly that. It would be quite an achievement, since our average selling year with the XJS was about 4500 cars. Our plans are to sell 7000 XK8s in the first full year, of which we expect about 70% to be the Convertible. With the XJS the Coupé wasn't even sold in the US towards the end – we only sold one in the '96 model year and that went 'in-house' to William Clay Ford.

"In the US the XK8 Coupé is acceptable to a much wider audience than the XJS. It's a little taller, a little wider and has more space inside – Americans tend to be

THE NEW JAGUAR XK8: THE CAT IS BACK

Core Communication Idea:

The communication idea revolves around a deliberate juxtaposition of the XK8 with the Jaguar animal.
It is an animal to be both feared and admired... powerful yet refined beneath its beautiful, sleek skin... a beast to be tamed.
Above all, it is a modern expression of the animal essence of everything that makes a jaguar like no other car.

rather larger than Europeans. Its styling is quite different from the Convertible, particularly when the Convertible has its soft-top up. The strength of the Convertible, though, is that we have concentrated on making it practical as well as beautiful. We have the largest trunk [boot] in class and a much cleaner line than our rivals. The beautiful thing about this soft-top, compared with any of our competitors, is that it has a heated glass backlight, which is very important in the US.

"In terms of sound deadening – wow. The XK8 is quieter than certainly any convertible in the marketplace at the moment. You simply don't need the hard-top that you get with the Mercedes – the car's winter-proof as it is. The XK8 Convertible is actually quieter than the XJS Coupé! So we've made a very multi-purpose car, and I think that sheer practicality is very strong selling point.

"The world is very competitive in North America. For the first few months people are going to kill to get an XK8. But in the end what's going to make this a good car is the styling, which has a lot of life in it. It has a quality that Jaguars have always had – dignity. It's not just a flashy shape, like a Corvette.

"But its other attributes are going to keep it selling – its smoothness, the driveline, the suspension, the handling. We shall move on from people wanting an XK8 simply because of its enormous Jaguar desirability, and pass into a phase where people will say, 'Wow! It's wonderful to drive. It really works. It has astonishing quality'. There'll also be great customer surprise at how practical the car is, and that'll sustain it."

THE XK8 IN DETAIL

Like its great ancestor, the XK120, the XK8 has a Jaguar 'Growler' badge on the nose.

The XK8 has a steel monocoque body with an entirely new superstructure consisting of 30% fewer panels than the XJS but providing 25% greater torsional stiffness. Overall length has been reduced to 15ft 7in (4.760m), width (excluding mirrors) increases to 6ft 0in (1.829m) and headroom is improved by 1.3in (33mm) in the

Coupé and 1.4in (35mm) in the Convertible. The colour-keyed bumpers consist of polyurethane injection-moulded covers mounted on thermoplastic beams. For North American specification cars the covers are mounted to aluminium beams connected to energy-absorbing struts. Front and rear screens are direct glazed.

Side light, dipped beam, main beam and direction indicator are combined in one integral unit which uses projector technology with a clear lens. The inside surface of this lens has a coat of nickel/chrome 'spluttering' to give a jewel-like appearance, and there is a micro-metric adjustment scale for beam alignment.

The headlamp power wash is concealed behind a small chrome panel which is flush with the lens. When activated by pressing the screen washer button, the nozzle extends 3in (75mm) telescopically and sprays the headlamp with a 0.4sec pulse. A second pulse of the same duration is repeated after 3secs. The headlamp wash only operates when the side lights – or dipped beam when daytime running lights are fitted – are on and at every sixth operation of the screen washers.

The AJ-V8 engine has a vee angle of 90 degrees, and bore and stroke dimensions of 86mm x 86mm give a displacement of 3996cc. The compression ratio is 10.75:1. The block and bed plate are die-cast aluminium alloy, and the bores are Nikasil-plated. The precision sand-cast aluminium alloy head features four valves per cylinder and pent-roof combustion chambers with twin overhead camshafts per bank. Variable Cam Phasing (VCP) improves exhaust emissions, idle stability and high-speed performance, and actually increases low-speed torque. Other significant features are aluminium tappets and 5mm valve stems. The AJ-V8 Engine Management System (EMS) has been developed specifically for Jaguar by Nippondenso. It controls fuelling, ignition, emission strategies and on-board diagnostics. The Engine Control Module (ECM) is the heart of the EMS and controls the electronic fuel injection – with eight sequentially-driven side-feed injectors – and the electronic ignition control, with spark energy developed by eight on-plug coils. The electronic throttle controls idle speed, cruise control, power limitation (engine protection), vehicle speed limiting, traction control, catalyst warm-up, mapped throttle progression and driveline shunt damping.

Designed to achieve very fast warm-up, even metal temperatures and increased bore temperatures, the cooling system employs a patented longitudinal flow regime along the block with 50% of the flow bypassing the bores. The unusually small coolant capacity is 42% lower than on the Lexus V8.

The ZF 5HP24 electronically-controlled automatic transmission has five speeds – a first for Jaguar. The

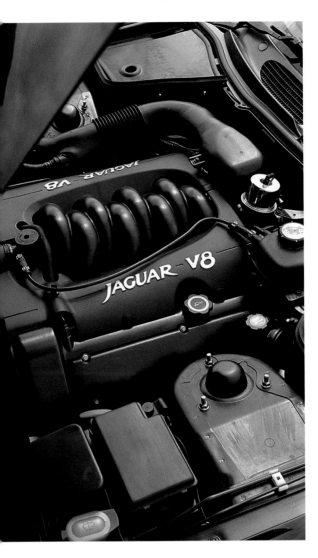

enhancing effect of the torque converter. Like the saloons, the gear selector lever is in a J-gate configuration. On the right are P, R, N, D (all gears). By moving the lever to the left from the D position, the ranges 4, 3 and 2 may be selected.

The prop shaft is a one-piece, hollow, lightweight, aluminium design of 4in (100mm) diameter which attaches to an all-new GKN 14HU differential with the pinion on both the engine crankshaft and vehicle centre line. The final drive ratio is 3.06:1.

The exhaust system incorporates integral downpipe catalysts coated with palladium and rhodium for very fast 'light-up'. The system converges into a single under-floor silencer and then splits into a twin system with intermediate silencers, over-axle pipes and rear silencer. Japanese specification cars are fitted with grass heatshields over the downpipe catalyst. Cars for North America have Exhaust Gas Recirculation (EGR).

The fuel tank is mounted above the rear suspension – a well-protected location in crash situations. A single fuel pump is located in the tank, whose capacity of 16.5

The heart of the XK8 is the new 4-litre, 32-valve V8 engine which produces 290bhp at 6100rpm and, thanks to all-aluminium construction, weighs just 441lb (200kg).

Side light, dipped beam, main beam and direction indicator are combined in one integral unit which uses projector technology with a clear lens. The inside surface of this lens has a coat of nickel/chrome 'spluttering' to give a jewel-like appearance.

gearshift points are selected by the Transmission Control Module (TCM) as a function of speed, engine load, selector position, throttle pedal movement, kickdown and mode switch. The transmission has seven shift programmes, including driver-switchable Normal or Sport modes. Other programmes include Cruise Control, which reduces unwanted hunting of the transmission; Traction Programme, which automatically changes gear when necessary to optimise traction and reduce wheelspin; Gradient Programme, which is implemented when the TCM detects that the car is climbing or is heavily laden; Warm-Up Mode, which holds lower gears when the engine is first started to facilitate the achievement of engine operating temperature to reduce emissions; and Hot-Mode Programme, which acts to minimise the amount of heat generated by the transmission when the fluids exceed a set temperature. Pressures adapt to changing characteristics due to ageing. The transmission is a fill-for-life unit and thus has no dipstick.

The torque converter clutch is engaged by the TCM as a function of throttle position, output speed, oil temperature, gear selection and shift programme. The clutch is disengaged prior to a downshift to utilise the comfort-

Imperial gallons (19.9 US gallons or 75.5 litres) gives a range of 437 miles (703km).

The independent front suspension is of a double wishbone design with the spring co-axial with the damper. The system design achieves almost 100% Ackerman geometry; both front wheels describe the radius on which they are travelling, thereby reducing tyre scrub. There is lower offset and increased castor in comparison with the XJS. The turning circle is reduced from the XJS's 13.0m to 11.0m and the cartridge wheel bear-

The headlamp power wash is concealed behind a small chrome panel which is flush with the lens. When activated by the screen washer button, the nozzle extends 3in (75mm) telescopically and sprays the headlamp.

ings are greased for life. The front cross-member is a light aluminium casting and the road springs are mounted direct to the body to reduce lower wishbone loads, improve wheel-to-spring ratio and aid 'hydramount' tuning. A one-piece anti-roll bar is fitted.

Fully independent rear suspension is shared with the XJ6 saloons. It has double wishbones incorporating the drive shafts as upper links. The wishbones are designed for anti-squat under acceleration and anti-lift under braking. A monostrut and a rear anti-roll bar are fitted as standard.

An optional package known as Computer Active Technology Suspension (CATS) is available for the Coupé only. Active-Controlled Dampers (ACD) are used and, under the control of an ECU, automatically select the best characteristics to suit the driving conditions, improving ride and handling. Uprated springs and 18in wheels are part of this package.

The ZF Servotronic rack and pinion power-assisted steering has three major elements. The hydraulic valve system gives variable effort dependent upon road speed. The rack has a variable ratio to provide 'quicker' steering off-centre, reducing the number of turns required at parking speeds and also sharpening the response to driver input at higher speeds. The number of turns lock to lock is 2.8. A Positive Centre Feel (PCF) torsion bar assists straight-line feel and precision, improving vehicle behaviour in cross-winds.

Ventilated 28mm x 305mm brake discs are fitted all round and the split-circuit braking system is vacuum-assisted. The sill-mounted handbrake lever has been redesigned with a lower height to improve entry and exit from the car, and the forward end curves down to avoid being caught in trouser turn-ups, shoes and skirts! Anti-lock braking is provided by the Teves Mk20 system,

'Seven-spoke' wheels of 18in diameter are optional with the normal suspension, but standard with the extra-cost CATS suspension. Different widths are used front and rear, and the front tyres are uni-directional.

The driver's seat has switches to alter height, fore/aft adjustment, lumbar support and angle of recline.

which comprises an hydraulic control unit with integral electronic controller and four wheel-speed sensors.

Stability Control is fitted to all cars and controlled by the engine management ECU. If a wheel spins, the ECU retards the ignition and backs off the electronic throttle to reduce power. Traction Control is also standard in most markets and additionally activates the ABS system and brakes the spinning wheel. Both systems can be switched off to suit conditions.

Alloy five-spoke 8J x 17in wheels are fitted with 245/50 ZR 17 Pirelli P ZERO asymmetric-tread tyres. With the CATS sports suspension, seven-spoke 8J x 18in wheels are fitted to the front and 9J x 18in to the rear. These are equipped with 245/45 ZR 18 Pirelli P ZERO directional-tread tyres at the front and 255/45 ZR 18 Pirelli P ZERO asymmetric-tread tyres at the rear. With this option a 3.5J x 18in space-saver wheel with a 135/80 R18 tyre is fitted as the spare. The jack and wheel brace are located with the spare wheel in a polythene tray under the boot floor.

Two interior styles are being offered, namely Sport and Classic (see panels for details). The standard driver's seat has electrical adjustment of fore/aft, recline, height rise/fall (UK/Europe only) and lumbar features. The standard passenger seat has the same features, except that height rise/fall is optional in all markets. Heated seats and two-position driver seat memory are also options. The seat controls are located on the outboard front edge of the seat cushion. Fixed rear seats are similar in style to the front seats.

The full-width fascia has a soft-feel grained surface, with the top a darker contrast colour to the lower part to reduce reflections in the windscreen. Mounted to the fascia are the air conditioning vents, instrument pack, centre console switch pack, air conditioning control panel,

SPORT TRIM	CLASSIC TRIM
* Charcoal fascia, door casings and quarter casings * Trim colour inserts in door casings * Charcoal twin-needle stitching on door armrest, seat and centre console/lid * Seat style with three horizontal flutes * Two cloth and three perforated leather colours available * Grey-stained bird's-eye maple veneer * Charcoal perforated leather gear knob * Charcoal perforated leather steering wheel	* Colour-coded contrast-colour fascia, steering wheel and door top rolls * Seat style with five vertical flutes * Five plain leather colours available * Burr walnut veneer * Half wood (to match walnut) and colour-keyed steering wheel * Wood gear knob to match walnut * No contrast stitching

The Sport interior has grey stained maple veneer on the main dashboard, centre console and door switch packs. On the Sport models the steering wheel is covered completely in leather, as is the gear knob; a half grey wood/half charcoal leather wheel is an option. The centre instrument pack comprises the oil pressure gauge (left), clock (centre) and battery indicator (right). Below the climate control panel is a row of switches that, depending on market, can include headlamp levelling adjustment, left- and right-hand seat heaters, front and rear fog lamps, traction control 'off' switch and hazard warning lights.

The Classic interior uses burr walnut, a half wood/half leather steering wheel and wooden gear knob to match the veneer. The main instruments, from left, are the rev counter (red-lined at 6800rpm), 170mph (280kph) speedometer, and combined fuel and temperature gauges. Within the speedometer a message pack, which shows the odometer reading in default, can display in 11 languages.

The Convertible soft-top can be lowered in less than 20 seconds and is operated by one hold-down switch. When being raised, the soft-top power-latches to the header rail to complete the operation entirely automatically, unlike on the XJS.

When the engine is started and the gearshift is moved out of Park, the car's doors automatically lock and the interior door handle physically moves into its cavity (in most markets). If the optional seat memory is fitted, the controls are located ahead of the handle. The steering wheel centre houses the driver's airbag and horn switch, and on either side are switches for the audio unit (left) and optional cruise control (right).

audio head unit and scuttle casings. Within the speedometer is a message pack that shows the odometer reading in default, and can display in English, American English, French, German, Italian, Spanish, Dutch, Swedish, Finnish, Japanese and Brazilian Portuguese. On the driver's side are switches for boot and fuel filler release, valet switch, and stowage for sunglasses. In front of the passenger is an illuminated, lockable glovebox with damped-action lid and a stowage shelf for the handbook.

The centre console contains the J-gate gear selector and, within the surround, switches for cruise control and gearbox mode. Behind these is the illuminated smoker's compendium. To the front is a shallow trinket tray with coin slots. On Convertible models the left-hand coin slots are replaced by the soft-top operation switch. There is a console cubby box, with optional cup-holder.

To the front of the door armrests are located the window switches, with two on the driver's side together with the power mirror controls. The seat memory switches, when applicable, are positioned at the front of the door handle bezel. On the front lower area of the door is a speaker (one of several) concealed by acoustic cloth.

The steering column is manually adjustable as standard, but there is also an optional electrically adjustable column that is fitted as standard for North America and certain other markets. This electric column is only offered with the driver memory feature and, apart from memory of column position, includes an automatic tilt-away facility for ease of entry and exit. An airbag is fitted to the steering wheel centre pad, which doubles as the

horn push on all cars. A passenger airbag is also standard.

The Climate Control System includes twin blowers. The electronic control panel consists of Centigrade/Fahrenheit selection, heated front (optional) and rear screen switches, and defrost switch, and displays digital temperature, manual fan speed level and external temperature. Air-flow is compensated for vehicle speed.

The Convertible soft-top is fully lined and has a die-cast aluminium frame designed to give a low stack-height when folded. A heated glass rear screen is standard. Soft-top operation, which includes a new power-latching feature for the final attachment to the windscreen header rail, is accomplished by a fully sealed electro-hydraulic system, and the entire cycle of stowage or erection, operated by a hold-down switch, takes less then 20 seconds. An audible tone sounds when the switch is pressed and first of all the rear side windows retract; when these windows are fully lowered, the soft-top is unlatched and folds back; the audible tone sounds again when the operation is complete. The soft-top can be operated on the move at speeds up to 10mph. A soft-top cover is supplied.

On all models the windows automatically drop 15mm when a door is opened and return to the 'up' position when the door is closed, assuming the window has not been lowered by an occupant. This enables the glass to lock into a U-shaped seal, resulting in improved weather sealing and reduced wind noise.

The XK8 electrical system is based on multiplexing rather than a traditional wiring harness. A network of electronic modules operates features by low-current switching. The body system consists of six modules. The powertrain and chassis electronic modules are grouped together in a Controller Area Network (CAN) and handle engine management, transmission control, ABS and the instrument cluster.

The remote transmitter has four buttons. One operates locking (the doors are deadlocked if it is pressed twice) and security arming. The second unlocks the doors (in North America the driver's door if pressed once, the passenger's door as well if pressed twice) and disarms the security system. The third switches on the headlamps for 25 seconds, or until pressed again. The fourth releases the boot.

Service intervals are 12 months or 10,000 miles (12,500 miles in the US), and there is an annual corrosion inspection. In the UK the mechanical and electrical warranty extends to three years or 60,000 miles, while the paint surface is covered for the same period but for an unlimited distance. In the US the XK8 is covered 'bumper-to-bumper' for four years or 50,000 miles. Resistance to body perforation through corrosion is guaranteed for six years and an unlimited mileage.

X100 97MY

The standard paint colours for the 1997 Model Year (ie, launched October 1996), from top left: Aquamarine, Topaz, British Racing Green, Sherwood Green, Anthracite, Carnival, Spindrift, Antigua, Titanium, Sapphire and Ice Blue.

PAINT COLOURS

Solid
British Racing Green
Spindrift *(white)*
Metallic
Sapphire *(dark blue)*
Ice Blue
Topaz
Micatallic
Carnival *(red)*
Titanium *(dark grey)*
Sherwood *(dark green)*
Anthracite *(black)*
Aquamarine *(light green)*
Antigua *(electric blue)*

CONVERTIBLE TOP

Beige *(N. America only)*
Blue
Black
Stone *(pale beige)*
Dark Green *(UK, Europe & Overseas only)*

ENGINE

Type AJ-V8
Cylinders 8
Configuration 90 degree V8
Displacement 3996cc (243.9cu in)
Bore x stroke 86mm x 86mm (3.386in x 3.386in)
Compression ratio 10.75:1
Maximum power 290bhp (294 DIN PS, 216Kw) @ 6100rpm
Maximum torque 290lb ft (393Nm) @ 4250rpm
Combustion chamber Pent roof
Valves per cylinder 4
Fuel grade 95 RON
Fuel system Electronic injection
Ignition system Nippondenso EMS with on-plug coils
Weight (dressed) 200kg (441lb)

CHASSIS

Wheel type/size Alloy 8J x 17in
Tyre size 245/50 ZR17
Braking system Teves ABS Mark 20
Steering ZF PAS with variable ratio
Turning circle 36ft 2in (11.0m)
Front suspension Fully independent with unequal length upper and lower wishbones mounted to fully isolated front cross beam; arranged to provide anti-dive under braking; coil springs, telescopic dampers and anti-roll bar
Rear suspension Fully independent double wishbone type system incorporating drive shafts acting as upper links; wishbones designed for anti-squat and anti-lift under acceleration and braking; concentric coil springs, dampers and anti-roll bar

BODY

Construction
All steel monocoque with front and rear crumple zones including front crash tubes; wrap-round protective bumpers

Paint & protection
Box sections and closed members hot wax injected; cathodic electrocoat; clear over base paint process with automated electrostatic application of primer/ sealer and clear coats; colour matched primer coat; twin colour coats; PVC underseal

Drag coefficient
Coupé   Convertible
0.35   0.36

INTERIOR TRIM

Cloth
(Sport - UK, Europe & Overseas only)
Oatmeal
Warm Charcoal
Embossed Leather
(Sport - UK, Europe & Overseas only)
Oatmeal
Warm Charcoal
Cream
Plain leather
(Classic)
Oatmeal
Warm Charcoal
Cream
Teal *(UK, Europe, & Overseas only)*
Coffee *(N. America only)*

TRANSMISSION

Type ZF 5HP24 5-speed automatic
Torque converter With slip-controlled lock-up clutch
Lubrication system Maintenance-free
Weight (with oil) 95kg (209lb)
Gear ratios
1st, 3.571:1
2nd, 2.200:1
3rd, 1.505:1
4th, 1.000:1
5th, 0.803:1
Reverse, 4.063:1
Final drive ratio 3.06:1
Mph per 1000rpm in top 32mph

PERFORMANCE

0-30mph
Coupé   Convertible
2.8sec   2.9sec
0-60mph
6.5sec   6.8sec
0-100kph
6.8sec   7.2sec
Maximum speed
156mph   154mph
(251kph) (248kph)
Fuel economy
Urban
15.7mpg 15.9mpg
Extra Urban
31.0mpg 32.1mpg
Combined
23.0mpg 23.3mpg

DIMENSIONS

Overall length
Coupé   Convertible
15ft 7in   15ft 7in
(4.760m) (4.760m)
Overall width
6ft 0in   6ft 0in
(1.829m) (1.829m)
Overall height
4ft 3in   4ft 3.5in
(1.296m) (1.306m)
Boot volume
327 litres 307 litres
Fuel tank capacity
75.5 litres 75.5 litres
Kerb weight
1649kg   1743kg
(3635lb) (3842lb)

THE CAT IS BACK

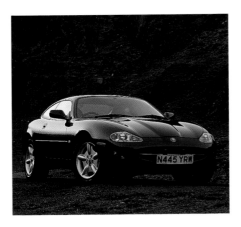

Through the fifties and sixties, Jaguar's stock was on the up and up. In the seventies, due mainly to external influences, it plunged. During the early-to-mid eighties the company's fortunes took a turn for the better, with privatisation, increasing sales and, in 1986, the launch of the all-important new saloon, codenamed XJ40. Profitability, aided in part by a favourable currency situation, rose to record levels. However, although major strides were made on quality, Jaguar still trailed its German competition, while Japanese entry in to the luxury sector was imminent.

Towards the end of the eighties, Jaguar faced an uncertain future. Luxury markets were contracting due to world-wide recession, the prospect of the British Government relinquishing the Golden Share would pave the way for a possible take-over, and there was inadequate funding for investment in new models.

The Ford take-over upset many die-hard enthusiasts from an emotional standpoint. Almost without exception, people feared the worst – the end of Jaguar's identity, character and independence. But Ford was more intelligent than that. As Nick Scheele says, "Of the £1.6 billion Ford spent, £1.3 billion was for the name. So Ford has been very conscious that the last thing it wanted to do was jeopardise the name."

Even so, the challenge was greater than even Ford realised. Ford discovered a great talent base, but a lack of direction. The ability was there throughout the company but it needed harnessing in a disciplined way, and the company desperately required an injection of funds to realise its ambitions. Starved of investment, the plants were archaic and had working practices to match. The company was a microcosm of industrial Britain, pre-Thatcher.

As we have seen, Ford carried out massive surgery to the patient – and the patient began to recover. With the launch of the new saloon, X300, it showed it could walk again, and walk tall. With the launch of the XK8, the former patient is running. But the important thing is that the patient's character has not changed at all. It is the same person, but that person is now healthy again and much stronger. It may sound over-dramatic, but Jaguar nearly had to die to live.

"To me, as an old Jaguar person," states US Jaguar President Mike Dale, "I can't think of a single mis-step the Ford management has made with Jaguar. In fact, quite the opposite. They have demonstrated an ability to help us where we desperately needed help, without crushing the Jaguar spirit. That would have been easy to do, because we're a mouse and they're an elephant, and even a friendly elephant can roll over on a mouse!"

It would be over-simplifying this story not to acknowledge that Jaguar's learning curve has been a steep and at times painful one. The gestation of the XK8 has not been a painless one either, but the spirit and ability have gelled to demolish every obstacle. Claims have been made in the past that Jaguar had turned the corner, but in truth it was not so. Now, thanks to Ford, performance can be measured. Art and science have been married.

The truly breathtaking scenery of mid-Wales, with its quiet roads and delightful lanes, is a perfect place to discover the Jaguar XK8

Very good protection from the elements is provided by the large, well raked windscreen, and one can drive in rain without suffering much. Turbulence, which can be so tiring in an open car, is significant by its absence.

"Ford pushed us to make good quality motor cars," says Paul Stokes. "They pushed us to get process control and financial discipline into this company, which for many people, me included, was an awakening. After acquisition, we were open enough to say, 'You're absolutely right. This is crazy. Why the hell have we been doing this?' They were hard lessons. It was, 'Run it on programme. Run it on budget. What's your quality target? What are warranty numbers going to be?' Bill Hayden was masterful. 'Show me the data. Where is it?'"

"We adopted World Class Timing," states Jim Padilla proudly, "on which Ford had benchmarked the world. Frankly, because Jaguar is a small, tight-knit team, we knew we could deploy it faster than Ford Motor Company – so we did."

Mike Beasley is the longest-serving Jaguar Director: "We pushed for change to get this ethos of continuous improvement. We pushed the thing along for 18 months, nearly two years, like pushing a boulder uphill. Then we hit some form of cusp point and the boulder started rolling along itself. It gathered speed. Everybody everywhere was very motivated and going very quickly indeed, getting teams together, making improvements. And management were running like crazy to keep up with the guys on the shop floor. That happened about

three years ago and was probably the best feeling of my entire career."

The engineers, led by Clive Ennos, are very positive: "We have one of the best engineering centres in the world – I really believe that. As a tight-knit unit, this really does take some beating."

The chimneys are gone and Roger Putnam no longer calls Whitley 'The Bunker': "Whereas XJ41 slipped a year every year and XJ40 was four years late, since Ford's arrival we've met every launch date on time, on volume, on price. The change in the company is just amazing."

Jim Padilla, the architect of a good deal of that change, is very impressed: "The X300 product, right now, is achieving the highest satisfaction ratings in the whole of the Ford Motor Company fleet. That's really pleasing. We used to be on page two – now we're top of page one. The people at Ford love Jaguar products. Yes, they drive them – the biggest fleet of Jaguars in the world today is at Ford World Headquarters. No question about it – they've all been dying to get their hands on an XK8. They want Jaguar to be a winner."

The atmosphere at Jaguar has been transformed, according to Helen Atkins: "I know we're biased, but everybody here just loves the car. People often stop you and ask, 'How's X100 going? What happened when they

the new Jaguar. Many of the suppliers have liaison engineers over here, and they're all very enthusiastic because it's Jaguar."

Jaguar styling probably stirs the blood more than any other part of the character. Geoff Lawson gives his conclusions: "We think we have a car that's in the spirit and tradition of Jaguar's great sports cars. Achieving that was very important to us."

Tony Duckhouse of Finance: "I own an E-type and I like sports cars – we all do. I found it useful to go down to the styling room every so often to remind myself of the emotional side of what we were doing, because if you're not careful the whole job becomes financial figures. But I'd go down there and think, 'This is a winner'. I'd look at the car and know that people are going to want to buy it – that keeps you motivated."

Clive Ennos: "One of the things you have to fight is the fact that you see any new car so early on and get used to it. I still get a buzz when I walk into the studio and see it."

Roger Putnam thinks the momentum can only get stronger: "I think in particular with the X300, and with the Series III saloon before that, the car looked better every time you saw it. The XJ40 didn't quite have that: it tended to look more slab-sided and older as you saw it. I've no doubt that XK8 has that magic of looking better each time you see it on the road."

Geoff Lawson again: "We can gauge if people's reaction to the style is sincere. Everybody who sees the XK8 loves it. They want one. 'When can I have one?' The cheque books come out. There's spontaneous applause."

But the XK8 is not just a beauty, as Bob Dover is keen to stress: "I think there's an important question – can you use it for business? With some of the little two-seaters like the Mazda Miata, the Mercedes SLK, the Porsche Boxster, I think the answer is probably 'no'. But when you have a decent amount of boot space, which is important to Jaguar customers in their day to day life,

took it to the autobahn tests? How's it going in the wind tunnel?' It's a great feeling to have worked on the car."

The enthusiasm extends to the suppliers, as Kevin Riches explains: "They want us to beat Lexus and Mercedes. I think they see us as a niche market, but traditionally British. They're so keen to get things right for

'Some are born great, some achieve greatness, and some have greatness thrust upon them,' wrote William Shakespeare. Jaguar sports cars are born great and the XK8 is no exception.

Sisters in spirit: it seems extraordinary that 35 years separate the XK8 from the E-type.

and what they want to do at the weekend, it's extremely important to be able to answer 'yes' to that question."

Nick Scheele agrees: "There are people who really want to be able to go away with a partner for a weekend and put in some luggage and maybe a set of golf clubs. That can't be done in a Porsche or Mercedes SL today because there isn't enough boot space. For me, the defining difference between a sports car – and I do love driving some of the sports cars – is that after you've hammered away for two hours, you get out and you feel your liver or your kidneys starting to react. What we need to do is provide a car you can drive for 10 hours and get out completely fresh. It goes back to the classic London to Monte Carlo run, and you can't do that in today's sports cars."

Bob Dover again: "Paul Walker's team worked long and hard to make the car very agile in the way it responds. The other thing is the power train. That team did an outstanding job on the torque of the engine, and the combination of that and the automatic transmission is just tremendous."

Refinement is also exceptional, as Mike Beasley underlines. "I've driven early prototypes that were a lot better for refinement than some of the production Jaguars I drove 15 years ago. Very pleasing for refinement, ride and handling, and NVH – the XK8 is a super car to drive. We have a real winner. If you have an exciting car that performs, rides and handles exceptionally

well, and we make it consistently, we are going to have a lot of satisfied customers."

Roger Putnam has occupied one of the hottest seats in the British motor industry for many years. The competition Jaguar will face in the coming years will be intense, but now he is leading the troops forward instead of merely trying to hold ground. With the XJ6 reborn and selling well, the XK8 unleashed and the higher-volume smaller saloons to come, together with other exciting cars in the more distant future, his task now is to work closely with the dealerships. They in their turn have had a tough time with lower sales until recently and, perversely, vastly improved quality means less business for the workshops.

"The end game as we launch the XK8 is actually getting the market ready for X200," says Putnam. "But the XK8 plays a crucial role in maintaining the momentum created with X300. Rather as they did in the eighties, dealers are again going to have to make a tremendous leap of faith to invest in new premises. To put a ballpark figure on it, between 1996 and 1998 our importers and dealers world-wide are going to have to invest another billion pounds in facilities to prepare themselves for the existence of the XK8 and the arrival of X200.

"The XK8 has been launched into a market that is changing. During the recession of the late eighties and early nineties, the structure of the car market, in our sectors, changed massively. It's very easy to suggest that the luxury sectors collapsed, but in fact they changed shape. If you were to add back all the expensive 4x4s and people carriers into the total, the market didn't collapse – it just changed.

"At the same time, there was a virtual collapse of the sports car market. The smaller cars like the Mazda MX5, the Japanese Lotus Elan, did very well. The more expensive, brasher cars like the Mazda RX7, the Nissan 300ZX and the Mitsubishi 2000 really didn't prosper at all in many European markets, and ended up being withdrawn from sale. So the sports car market, as well, has changed shape – and the XK8 has been launched into a marketplace that is about to become incredibly competitive.

"But we never lose sight of one of Sir William Lyons' original tenets – Jaguar must offer value for money."

Mike Dale exudes infectious enthusiasm. "I feel that in leading Jaguar in North America, particularly in the final few years of my working life, the most important thing I must do is make sure that the group of younger people around me get passed on to them the passion for Jaguar, and the understanding of what that passion means. In listening to the customers, you can hear it. You almost get the feeling that if you don't make the company work, they're going to come after you! They love Jaguar so much.

"Now we're making very technically competitive cars, becoming far more price competitive, and our warranty costs are falling. For the first time, I think, in Jaguar's recent history, passion is going to be translated from a defensive emotion that keeps the company alive, to one that will set us apart from Mercedes-Benz and BMW.

"Listening to people speak about Jaguar fills you with a really profound feeling that there are certain marques in the world – Jaguar is clearly one, although I'm not very objective about it! – that must be treasured for no better reason than the fact that they add quality to life. When I get in a Jaguar to drive to work, I feel better. I enjoy the experience.

"I'm a machine person – I've sailed, I've motor raced and I've flown aeroplanes since I was 17 or 18. I sit in a Jaguar and start the engine. I know that I've awoken something. That's what this sports car is all about. We've tried so hard to make this a sports car that people will want when they see it. When they drive it, they'll buy it. But when they live with it, they'll grow to love it.

"XK8 is far more important to North America than its numbers would suggest. Passers-by will rub their noses against the windows on Sunday mornings to look inside. It's important as a car, but in fact the engine, long-term, may be even more important to us than the car itself. Technically the British motor industry over the past 25 years hasn't produced much, frankly, but our V8 engine is the best 4-litre engine, in my view, the world has ever seen. I say that because of its all-round excellence in emissions, fuel consumption, power and the fact that you can't fall below 80% of the torque regardless of speed.

"The XK8 is technically very competent against its competitors in terms of steering, braking, ride and handling, but all this only takes you to the starting line. The thing that makes the XK8 different is the sinuosity of the chassis, of the way everything blends together in a peculiarly silky Jaguar way."

Nick Scheele is equally excited: "I think we need a flagship. For me XK8 is the flagship. I think that's good for the dealers, the sales people, the customers, the service people – and most importantly youngsters throughout the world. I will never forget when I went up to college and saw my first E-type – red. It made such an incredible impression. Whereas previously I'd considered Jaguars somewhat staid, with models like the Mark X, all of a sudden I saw this E-type and it totally changed my perception of Jaguar as a company. I think XK8 can do the same today.

"We have all lived with the XK8 from its very earliest days. I think all of us were really delighted with Geoff's styling. It's simple and uncluttered – it harks back to the first E-type in having that same classically pure line.

"The engine and the power train in total have been a revelation. The refinement and the chassis solidity and the steering response are remarkable. The power of the brakes is astonishing. It's a very, very pleasing car. You feel you just want to go on driving and driving."

These are exciting times for Jaguar. The latest XJ6 saloon is selling extremely well and rebuilding the company and its reputation. The XK8 is once more giving Jaguar added zest and appeal to younger buyers. The foundations are in place for the launch of the much higher volume X200 smaller saloon in the late nineties, and there are even thoughts of a fourth string to the model range after that. This Jaguar renaissance will bring to fruition the original ambitions of Sir William Lyons, whose similarly structured range of cars built Jaguar's name in the fifties.

It could be said that, to a large extent, we all knew in principle what sort of sports car Jaguar should build. With a heritage as strong as the XKs and E-types, it was not difficult to see that the company had gone astray with the XJS, despite its commercial success after a hesitant start. In simplistic terms, it was not difficult to see how Jaguar could get back on track. The concept was clear, but the execution was the challenge for Bob Dover, the Project Team and their colleagues.

It has been no mean challenge. Indeed it was a daunting task to succeed such legendary cars, which set new standards in their time and which were clothed in bodies of outstanding, lasting beauty. The challenge was to perpetuate the performance and style that have made the name of Jaguar famous throughout the world.

Having driven the cars extensively, having bombarded many at Jaguar with probing questions, and having been party to all information, however sensitive, I firmly believe that Jaguar has indeed succeeded with the XK8. Another great Jaguar sports car has been unleashed.

The cat is back!

SIMULATORS

No	Reg no	Body	Vehicle type	Build dates	User area	Comment
1	H182FWK	Coupé	AJ26 Engine Simulator	4.93-6.93	Power train development	XJS Coupé modified to accept AJ26 engine
2		Conv	AJ26 Engine Simulator	5.93-8.93	Fuel & exhaust system development	XJS Convertible modified to accept AJ26 engine
3		Conv	AJ26 Engine Simulator	5.93-8.93	Engine management system development	XJS Convertible modified to accept AJ26 engine
4	K596KDU	Coupé	AJ26 Engine Simulator	11.92-3.93	Hot climate testing, Phoenix, Arizona	XJS Coupé modified to accept AJ26 engine
5		Conv	AJ26 Engine Simulator	11.92-2.93	Engine management system development	XJS Convertible modified to accept AJ26 engine
6	L968RVC	Conv	AJ26 Engine Simulator	2.93-4.93	Traction control development	XJS Convertible modified to accept AJ26 engine
7		Conv	AJ26 Engine Simulator	2.93-4.93	Electrical development	XJS Convertible modified to accept AJ26 engine
8	K190LHP	Coupé	AJ26 Engine Simulator	3.93-5.93	Exhaust development	XJS Coupé modified to accept AJ26 engine
9		Coupé	AJ26 Engine Simulator	4.93-6.93	High-speed testing, Pecos, USA	XJS Coupé modified to accept AJ26 engine
10		Conv	Driveline Simulator	4.93-7.93	Driveline development	XJS Convertible as engine Simulator, but with X100 rear axle
11		Coupé	Suspension Simulator	10.92-8.93	Chassis development	XJS Coupé modified to accept X100 front/rear suspensions, propshaft & AJ26 engine
12	K151GHP	Coupé	Suspension Simulator	11.92-7.93	Chassis development	XJS Coupé modified to accept X100 front/rear suspensions, propshaft & AJ26 engine
13		Coupé	Cooling Simulator	10.92-3.93	Cooling system development	XJS Coupé photographed by *Car* magazine at Nardo, summer 1993
14		Coupé	Seating/In-Car Entertainment Simulator		Seating & ICE development	XJS Coupé with X100 seats & stereo system
15		Coupé	Aerodynamic Simulator	11.92-1.93	Aerodynamic testing	Full-size GRP rolling bodyshell for wind tunnel evaluation
16		Saloon	Electrical Engine Management Simulator		Engine management development	XJ40 saloon fitted with AJ26 engine
17		Coupé	Front Crash Simulator	1.93-2.93	Frontal crash testing	XJS Coupé with front modified to X100 body structure & AJ26 engine model
18		Coupé	Front Crash Simulator	2.93-4.93	Frontal crash testing	XJS Coupé with front modified to X100 body structure & AJ26 engine model
19		Coupé	Front Crash Simulator	4.93-6.93	Frontal crash testing	XJS Coupé with front modified to X100 body structure & AJ26 engine model
20		Coupé	Side Crash Simulator	6.93-8.93	Side crash testing	Half-and-half XJS/X100 bodyshell
21		Conv	Side Crash Simulator	8.93-10.93	Side crash testing	Half-and-half XJS/X100 bodyshell
22		Coupé	Body/Security System Simulator		Electrical, body & security system	XJS Coupé with part X100 electrical system
23		Sal	Air Conditioning Development		Air conditioning defrost/demist	XJ40 saloon with windscreen modified to X100 rake angle
24		Coupé	Mobile Interior Ergonomic Buck		Interior ergonomics	X100 interior mock-up for ergonomic assessment
N/A		Buggy	Suspension Test Buggy		Suspension testing & development	Unique suspension test vehicle

MECHANICAL PROTOTYPES

No	Reg no	Body	Vehicle type	Build dates	User area	Comment
1		Coupé	Base Mechanical Prototype	10.93-11.93	Engine management system	XJS lookalike with X100 drivetrain (axles, propshaft & engine)
2		Coupé	Base Mechanical Prototype	11.93-12.93	Front suspension development	XJS lookalike with X100 drivetrain (axles, propshaft & engine)
3	L710VHP	Conv	Base Mechanical Prototype	10.93-12.93	Suspension mountings development	XJS lookalike with X100 drivetrain (axles, propshaft & engine)
4	L750WDU	Coupé	Base Mechanical Prototype	11.93-12.93	Engine management system	XJS lookalike with X100 drivetrain (axles, propshaft & engine)
6	M749GDU	Coupé	Base Mechanical Prototype	10.93-12.93	Brakes, ABS/traction control	XJS lookalike with X100 drivetrain (axles, propshaft & engine)
7	L749WDU	Coupé	Base Mechanical Prototype	11.93-12.93	Electrical, engine management system	XJS lookalike with X100 drivetrain (axles, propshaft & engine)
8		Coupé	Base Mechanical Prototype	12.93-1.94	Pavé structural test	XJS lookalike with X100 drivetrain (axles, propshaft & engine)
10		Coupé	Base Mechanical Prototype	2.94-3.94	Fuel & exhaust system development	XJS lookalike with X100 drivetrain (axles, propshaft & engine)
11		Coupé	Base Mechanical Prototype	2.94-3.94	Chassis, ride & handling	Vehicle written off, rolled during ride & handling testing
12	M694CRW	Conv	Base Mechanical Prototype	2.94-3.94	Chassis, ride & handling	XJS lookalike with X100 drivetrain (axles, propshaft & engine)
13	M64JRW	Coupé	Base Mechanical Prototype	2.94-3.94	Transmission development	XJS lookalike with X100 drivetrain (axles, propshaft & engine)
14	M785GDU	Coupé	Base Mechanical Prototype	12.93-1.94	Transmission development	XJS lookalike with X100 drivetrain (axles, propshaft & engine)
15	L745WDU	Coupé	Base Mechanical Prototype	12.93-1.94	Transmission software development	XJS lookalike with X100 drivetrain (axles, propshaft & engine)
16	L746WDU	Coupé	Base Mechanical Prototype	12.93-1.94	Engine management system	XJS lookalike with X100 drivetrain (axles, propshaft & engine)
17		Coupé	Base Mechanical Prototype	10.93-12.93	Cold & hot testing (Timmins & Phoenix)	XJS lookalike with X100 drivetrain (axles, propshaft & engine)
18	M689CRW	Coupé	Base Mechanical Prototype	10.93-12.93	Cold testing (Timmins) & electrical development	XJS lookalike with X100 drivetrain (axles, propshaft & engine)
19		Coupé	Air Conditioning Mechanical Prototype	5.93-9.93	Video & air conditioning testing	Running X100 lookalike in GRP, built on Simulator underframe
20	M748GDU	Coupé	Base Mechanical Prototype	3.94-4.94	Brakes, ABS/traction control	XJS lookalike with X100 drivetrain (axles, propshaft & engine)
21	M692CRW	Coupé	Base Mechanical Prototype	3.94-4.94	Brakes, foundation system	XJS lookalike with X100 drivetrain (axles, propshaft & engine)
22	M687CRW	Coupé	Base Mechanical Prototype	3.94-4.94	Power unit, city cycle & high speed	XJS lookalike with X100 drivetrain (axles, propshaft & engine)
23	M686CRW	Coupé	Base Mechanical Prototype	3.94-4.94	Vehicle Office development	XJS lookalike with X100 drivetrain (axles, propshaft & engine)
24	M693CRW	Coupé	Base Mechanical Prototype	12.93-1.94	Steering development (RHD)	XJS lookalike with X100 drivetrain (axles, propshaft & engine)
25	M696CRW	Coupé	Base Mechanical Prototype	3.94-4.94	Steering development (LHD)	XJS lookalike with X100 drivetrain (axles, propshaft & engine)
27		Coupé	Special Mechanical Prototype	11.94-12.94	NVH development	First representative X100 Coupé shape (later built into running vehicle)
28		Conv	Special Mechanical Prototype		NVH development	First representative X100 Convertible shape (non-runner, rear-end crash tested)
29		Coupé	Base Mechanical Prototype	3.94-4.94	Hot testing (Phoenix)	Written off after rear-end collision in Phoenix, Arizona
30		Coupé	Base Mechanical Prototype	3.94-4.94	Brakes, foundation system	XJS lookalike with X100 drivetrain (axles, propshaft & engine)
32		Conv	Front Crash Mechanical Prototype	1.94-3.94	Front crash testing	Modified base MP bodyshell with X100 front suspension & AJ26 engine model (non-runner)
33		Coupé	Front Crash Mechanical Prototype	9.93-1.94	Front crash testing	Modified base MP bodyshell with X100 front suspension & AJ26 engine model (non-runner)
34		Conv	Front Crash Mechanical Prototype	3.94-4.94	Front crash testing	Modified base MP bodyshell with X100 front suspension & AJ26 engine model (non-runner)
35		Coupé	Front Crash Mechanical Prototype	3.94-5.94	Front crash testing	Modified base MP bodyshell with X100 front suspension & AJ26 engine model (non-runner)
37		Conv	Front Crash Mechanical Prototype	4.94-6.94	Front crash testing	Modified base MP bodyshell with X100 front suspension & AJ26 engine model (non-runner)
39		Coupé	Side Crash Mechanical Prototype	12.93-2.94	Side crash testing	Left-hand side X100, right-hand side XJS (non-runner)
40		Conv	Side Crash Mechanical Prototype	12.93-2.94	Side crash testing	Left-hand side X100, right-hand side XJS (non-runner)
41		Coupé	Side Crash Mechanical Prototype	1.94-3.94	Side crash testing	Left-hand side X100, right-hand side XJS (non-runner)
42		Conv	Side Crash Mechanical Prototype	1.94-3.94	Side crash testing	Left-hand side X100, right-hand side XJS (non-runner)
43		Conv	Side Crash Mechanical Prototype	2.94-4.94	Side crash testing	Left-hand side X100, right-hand side XJS (non-runner)
44		Coupé	Sensor Calibration Mechanical Prototype	4.94-5.94	Airbag sensor calibration	Modified base MP bodyshell (X100 front end complete), X100 front suspension & AJ26 engine (non-runner)
45	M760GDU	Coupé	Base Mechanical Prototype	4.94-7.94	On-board diagnostics	XJS lookalike with X100 drivetrain (axles, propshaft & engine)
46		Conv	Sensor Calibration Mechanical Prototype	3.94-4.94	Airbag sensor calibration	Modified base MP bodyshell (X100 front end complete), X100 front suspension & AJ26 engine (non-runner)

No	Reg no	Body	Vehicle type	Build dates	User area	Comment
47		Conv	Sensor Calibration Mechanical Prototype	5.94-6.94	Airbag sensor calibration	Modified base MP bodyshell (X100 front end complete), X100 front suspension & AJ26 engine (non-runner)
48	M765GDU	Coupé	Base Mechanical Prototype	4.94-7.94	On-board diagnostics	XJS lookalike with X100 drivetrain (axles, propshaft & engine)
50		Conv	Sensor Calibration Mechanical Prototype	5.94-6.94	Airbag sensor calibration	Modified base MP bodyshell (X100 front end complete), X100 front suspension & AJ26 engine (non-runner)
51		Coupé	Sensor Calibration Mechanical Prototype	6.94-7.94	Airbag sensor calibration	Modified base MP bodyshell (X100 front end complete), X100 front suspension & AJ26 engine (non-runner)
52	M766GDU	Coupé	Base Mechanical Prototype	4.94-7.94	On-board diagnostics	XJS lookalike with X100 drivetrain (axles, propshaft & engine)
53		Conv	Sensor Calibration Mechanical Prototype	6.94-7.94	Airbag sensor calibration	Modified base MP bodyshell (X100 front end complete), X100 front suspension & AJ26 engine (non-runner)

EVALUATION PROTOTYPES

No	Reg no	Body	Vehicle type	Build dates	User area	Comment
1		Coupé	Evaluation Prototype	1.95-2.95	Engine management system	
2		Coupé	Evaluation Prototype	1.95-2.95	Jaguar diagnostics dystem	
3		Coupé	Evaluation Prototype	11.94-12.94	Electrical development	Front end damage at MIRA (struck trackside pole) – repaired
4		Coupé	Evaluation Prototype	1.95-2.95	Power unit development, Timmins & Phoenix	
5	M992JKV	Conv	Evaluation Prototype	12.94-1.95	Engine management system	
6		Conv	Evaluation Prototype	12.94-1.95	Electrical development	Sustained accident damage at MIRA (front & rear) – repaired
7		Conv	Evaluation Prototype	11.94-12.94	Engine management system	Frontal damage in workshop – repaired
8		Coupé	Evaluation Prototype	10.94-11.94	Power unit development, Timmins	First running X100 Coupé – build completed in 21 days
9	M994JKV	Coupé	Evaluation Prototype	2.95	Hot room tests	Sustained rear damage while road testing – repaired
11		Coupé	Evaluation Prototype	2.95	Wiper & washer development	
12		Coupé	Evaluation Prototype	12.94-1.95	Air conditioning development	Air conditioning testing, Timmins, winter 1994/95
13		Conv	Evaluation Prototype	1.95-2.95	Phoenix hot testing	
14		Coupé	Evaluation Prototype	2.95-3.95	Seals development	Used in wind tunnel for wind noise testing
15		Coupé	Evaluation Prototype	2.95-3.95	Transmission development	
17		Coupé	Evaluation Prototype	10.94-11.94	Air conditioning development	Shipped to Nippondenso, Japan
18		Conv	Evaluation Prototype	1.95	PASCAR structural test	Completed PASCAR test & reshelled with spare EP body for further test
20	M993JKV	Coupé	Evaluation Prototype	2.95-3.95	Cooling development, Nardo	Photographed at Nardo, summer 1995
22		Conv	Evaluation Prototype	1.95-2.95	Convertible soft-top/seals development	Used in wind tunnel for wind noise testing
24		Conv	Evaluation Prototype	10.94-11.94	Power unit development, Timmins	Went from Timmins to Nippondenso, Japan
25	M532ODU	Coupé	Evaluation Prototype	2.95-4.95	Vehicle Office, whole vehicle development	Ride & Drive – JNA management, Mahwah & Jackie Stewart, Scotland
26	N976RKV	Conv	Evaluation Prototype	3.95-4.95	Vehicle Office, whole vehicle development	Ride & Drive – JNA management, Mahwah & Jackie Stewart, Scotland
31		Coupé	Evaluation Prototype	2.95-3.95	Noise, Vibration & Harshness development	Used to develop sound-deadening pack at Unikeller
32	M759GDU	Conv	Evaluation Prototype	12.95	Brake development	Brake testing, Sweden, winter 1994/95
33		Conv	Evaluation Prototype	10.94-11.94	Power unit development, Timmins & Phoenix	First running X100 Convertible – build completed in 11 days
36		Conv	Evaluation Prototype	2.95-3.95	Rear crash test	
37		Conv	Evaluation Prototype	2.95-3.95	Front crash test	
38		Coupé	Evaluation Prototype	2.95-3.95	Side crash test (non-runner)	
39		Conv	Evaluation Prototype	2.95-3.95	Side crash test (non-runner)	

VERIFICATION PROTOTYPES

No	Reg no	Body	Vehicle type	Build dates	User area	Comment
1		Coupé	Verification Prototype	10.95	Chassis development	
2		Conv	Verification Prototype	9.95	Electrical system sign-off	
3		Conv	Verification Prototype	11.95	Electrical, engine management system	
4		Coupé	Verification Prototype	12.95	Noise, Vibration & Harshness	
5	N257XDU	Coupé	Verification Prototype	11.95	Traction control/brakes development	Traction control testing, Sweden, winter 1995/96
8		Conv	Verification Prototype	11.95	Engine sign-off	
9		Coupé	Verification Prototype	9.95	Timmins & Phoenix tests	Timmins, winter 1995/96; Phoenix, summer 1996
10		Conv	Verification Prototype	10.95	Technical publications	
11		Conv	Verification Prototype	10.95	PASCAR structural test	
12		Coupé	Verification Prototype	9.95	Air conditioning tests	Timmins, winter 1995/96
14	N297XDU	Conv	Verification Prototype	10.95	Chassis development	Ride & Drive/Vehicle Assessment Group
15		Coupé	Verification Prototype	10.95	Seals & wind noise development	
16		Conv	Verification Prototype	11.95	Noise, Vibration & Harshness	
17		Coupé	Verification Prototype	10.95	Vehicle Engineering, whole vehicle development	
18		Conv	Verification Prototype	10.95	Seals & wind noise development	
19		Conv	Verification Prototype	9.95	Timmins & Phoenix tests	Timmins winter 1995/1996, Phoenix summer 1996
20	N298XDU	Coupé	Verification Prototype	11.95	Crash test	Ride & Drive/Vehicle Assessment Group
21		Coupé	Verification Prototype	11.95	Crash test	
22		Conv	Verification Prototype	11.95	Crash test	
28		Coupé	Verification Prototype	11.95	Crash test	
29		Conv	Verification Prototype	12.95	Crash test	
31		Coupé	Verification Prototype	11.95	Crash test	
32		Conv	Verification Prototype	11.95	Crash test	
33		Conv	Verification Prototype	12.95	Crash test	
34		Coupé	Verification Prototype	11.95	Crash test	
36		Coupé	Verification Prototype	12.95	Crash test	
38		Conv	Verification Prototype	12.95	PASCAR structural test	
50		Conv	Verification Prototype	12.95	PASCAR structural test	
51		Coupé	Verification Prototype	12.95	Vehicle Engineering evaluation	
52		Conv	Verification Prototype	1.96	Vehicle Engineering evaluation	
53		Conv	Verification Prototype	12.95	Vehicle Engineering evaluation (Launch Team)	
100		Coupé	Verification Prototype	1.96	Geneva Show Car	Reworked to design intent condition by Browns Lane Press Cars
101		Conv	Verification Prototype	1.96	New York Show Car	Reworked to design intent condition by Browns Lane Press Cars

GLOSSARY

AJ26 Codename for the new 4-litre Jaguar V8 engine, launched as AJ-V8.

Benchmark A point of reference from which measurements can be made; something that serves as a standard from which others may be measured.

Benchmarking The process that assesses characteristics of an organisation, product or process compared to similar processes elsewhere.

Body-in-White (BIW) The steel bodyshell of a motor vehicle while still in white metal state, before priming and painting.

Bucks Partial prototypes used to provide design perspective to aid all affected areas in finalising designs.

Chunk Teams Cross-functional, multi-skilled teams.

Clinic A marketing research project designed to measure consumer reaction to the styling of current and future products in comparison with competitors.

Computer Aided Design (CAD) Computer systems that have largely superseded conventional draughting techniques in the production of engineering design drawings, packaging and stress analysis work.

Computer Aided Manufacturing (CAM) The production of tooling or components directly from CAD tapes on the appropriate machine tools.

Computer Aided Engineering (CAE) The use of a computer, a set of programmes and analytical models to simulate the behaviour of a product or process, and then interpreting the results to predict if the process or product performs as designed.

Concept to Customer (CTC) A product delivery process, now superseded by WCT.

EP Evaluation Prototype.

FB Functional Build (also known as 1PP) serving as the first production prove-out.

FMEA Failure Mode and Effect Analysis.

4P Production prove-out ('For Production') using production parts and processes.

Gateways Review points at which the progress of a programme is assessed by senior management.

Go For One A major decision point where one of several alternatives is selected.

Hard Points Specified surfaces, lines, points or dimensions which define the dimensional limits guiding vehicle design.

Heavyweight Project Team A project team with members empowered by their home departments to make most of their own decisions for the department with respect to the project.

Iteration Repeated but modified version.

Job 1 The date the first saleable vehicle is loaded on to the Main Vehicle Assembly Track; with the XK8 this occurred on 4 June 1996.

Long-Lead Funding Funds for vendor tooling, or capital expenditure, that are needed prior to full programme funding release.

Metrics Measurements of performance which predict status of key parameters, against targets.

Model Stack A complete and highly stable model of the outer skin of a vehicle, built from dimensions taken directly from the approved styling clay model, and normally made from a special resin composite material.

MP Mechanical Prototype.

NovaC Quality audit.

NVH Noise, Vibration and Harshness.

PASCAR Structural and durability vehicle tests, title derived from 'Pass Car'.

Q1 Ford preferred quality award.

Ride and Drive A formal programme of vehicle assessment by committee, comparing Jaguar products with competitors.

VCP Variable Cam Phasing.

VP Verification Prototype.

World Class Timing (WCT) An enhanced product delivery process created in response to the competitiveness of Japanese quality and introduction lead-times.

X100 Internal codename for the XK8.

X200 Internal codename for the smaller sports saloon to be launched in the late nineties.

X300 Internal codename for the XJ saloons launched in 1994.

XJ40 Internal codename for the XJ saloons launched in 1986.